Developing Reading Comprehension Skills Years 5–6

Classic Children's Literature

Kate Heap

Publisher's information

We hope you and your pupils enjoy using the ideas in this book. Brilliant Publications publishes many other books to help primary school teachers. To find out more details on all of our titles, including those listed below, please go to our website: www.brilliantpublications.co.uk.

Books in the Developing Reading Comprehension Skills series:
- Classic Children's Literature Years 3-4
- Classic Children's Literature Years 5-6
- Classic Poetry Years 3-4
- Classic Poetry Years 5-6
- Contemporary Children's Literature Years 3-4
- Contemporary Children's Literature Years 5-6
- Non-fiction Years 3-4
- Non-fiction Years 5-6

Brilliant Activities for Reading Comprehension series
Getting to Grips with English Grammar series
Brilliant Activities for Creative Writing series
Brilliant Activities for Grammar and Punctuation series
Boost Creative Writing series

Published by Brilliant Publications Limited
Unit 10
Sparrow Hall Farm
Edlesborough
Dunstable
Bedfordshire
LU6 2ES, UK

www.brilliantpublications.co.uk

The name Brilliant Publications and the logo are registered trademarks.

Written by Kate Heap
Illustrated by Paula Martyr
Cover illustrated by Elizabeth May

© Brilliant Publications Limited 2021

Printed ISBN: 978-0-85747-837-5
ePDF ISBN: 978-0-85747-839-9

First printed in 2021

See page 181 for Acknowledgements.

The right of Kate Heap to be identified as the author of this work has been asserted by her in accordance with sections 77 and 78 of the Copyright, Designs and Patents Act 1988.

All rights reserved. Apart from any use permitted under UK copyright law, no part of this publication may be reproduced or transmitted in any form or by any means, electronic or mechanical, including photocopying and recording, or held within any information storage and retrieval system, without permission in writing from the publishers or under licence from the Copyright Licensing Agency Limited. Further details of such licenses (for reprographic reproduction) may be obtained from the Copyright Licensing Agency Limited, 5th Floor, Shackleton House, 4 Battle Bridge Lane, London SE1 2HX (https://cla.co.uk)

Dedication

Special thanks to the Year 6 children (2018-19) at Farsley Farfield Primary School for their encouragement and fantastic editorial advice and to Rob, Charlie, Lucy and Tom for always believing in me.

About the Author

Kate Heap

Kate has always loved books, her childhood overflowing with the adventures found within their pages. Now, as both a teacher and a parent, one of her greatest joys and privileges is sharing her love of literature with children.

Born and raised in Canada, Kate began her teaching career with Regina Public Schools. Ready for new adventures, she moved to the UK in 2001. Kate has spent many rewarding years in Leeds schools guiding children through the world of learning. She has supported primary school teachers through her roles of Literacy Leader, Leading Literacy Teacher for Leeds, Advanced Skills Teacher and Senior Leadership with responsibility for Assessment.

As a Primary English Consultant, Kate is now able to share her knowledge and enthusiasm even further. She enjoys reviewing children's literature for her blog, Scope for Imagination, working with authors and publishers to spread the word about their incredible books, and is passionate about helping teachers, parents and children find just the right ones for them. In her series, *Developing Reading Comprehension Skills*, Kate has created classroom resources that support both children and teachers in their quest to achieve key objectives and prepare for assessment while fostering a love of literature.

Kate is adventuring through life with her ever supportive husband, three wonderful children and two very special cats.

Contents

About the Author 1
Introduction 4–5
How to Use this Book 6–12
Reading Content Domain 8–12
    Vocabulary 8
    Retrieval 8
    Summary 9
    Inference 9
    Prediction 10
    Text Meaning 10
    Author's Use of Language 11
    Compare and Contrast 12
Little House in the Big Woods *by Laura Ingalls Wilder* 13–24
The Lion, the Witch and the Wardrobe *by C.S. Lewis* 25–36
Swallows and Amazons *by Arthur Ransome* 37–50
The Call of the Wild *by Jack London* 51–61
The Hobbit *by J.R.R. Tolkien* 62–72
Anne of Green Gables *by Lucy Maud Montgomery* 73–83
Black Beauty *by Anna Sewell* 84–94
The Secret Garden *by Frances Hodgson Burnett* 95–106
The Jungle Book *by Rudyard Kipling* 107–120
Treasure Island *by Robert Louis Stevenson* 121–131
Twenty Thousand Leagues Under the Sea *by Jules Verne* 132–145
A Christmas Carol *by Charles Dickens* 146–158

Answers 159–180
Acknowledgements 181
References 181

Introduction

Classic: Judged over a period of time to be of the highest quality and outstanding of its kind; a work of art of recognised and established value. (Oxford English Dictionary)

The world of classic children's literature is full of rich language and exciting adventures. Through these timeless stories, children are able to journey to worlds and times different from their own and lose themselves in the lives of unforgettable characters. Once children get a taste of these wonderful stories, they often want to read more and go on to experience books they may not otherwise discover. In these stories, they meet fascinating characters with whom they want to become life-long friends. Children soon realise that people are basically the same throughout history and that these characters want to be happy, find friends and be loved, just as they do.

In recent years, we have seen a number of changes to the Key Stage 2 English Curriculum, the Key Stage 2 Reading Test Framework and in the overall expectations for pupils. A focus on higher level vocabulary and increased use of more classic style texts and language has presented new challenges for both teachers and children.

It is essential that children are familiar with the wealth of classic children's literature from both Great Britain and around the world. The richness of language and the art of story telling provided by these types of texts allow children to expand their understanding of the world. They are then better able to make links between literature, history, geography, science and other areas.

In this book, children in Years 5–6 are exposed to a variety of these rich texts. They are given opportunities to tackle more complex vocabulary, develop endurance for longer passages and practise each of the eight reading content domain question types. It is also my hope that children will want to read on and have the opportunity to immerse themselves in some of the greatest stories ever written.

The texts selected for this book have been intentionally chosen to provide teachers with a variety of characters and settings. This broadens the range of children's reading and ensures there will be something of interest for every reader.

It is important to keep in mind that some classic texts include words or descriptions which, although considered appropriate or a part of everyday language at the time the books were originally published, are now considered inappropriate, stereotypical or even racist. Rather than throwing away these stories, it is important that teachers and parents address this with children. By discussing the culture and language at the time the book was written and how the world has changed, children will become aware of the development of language and respect for others. It is very important for children to understand and talk about why it is inappropriate to describe groups of people in stereotypical ways and for adults to help children to approach these older texts with sensitivity and awareness. These learning opportunities provide children with a chance to discuss how language evolves over time as inclusiveness, communities and cultures grow.

Main Characters in the Extracts	
<u>Female</u> Anne of Green Gables The Lion, the Witch and the Wardrobe Little House in the Big Woods The Secret Garden	<u>Male</u> The Hobbit Treasure Island 20,000 Leagues Under the Sea A Christmas Carol
<u>Both Boys and Girls</u> Swallows and Amazons	<u>Animals</u> Black Beauty The Jungle Book The Call of the Wild

Settings of the Extracts	
<u>Britain</u> The Lion, the Witch and the Wardrobe (English countryside) The Secret Garden (Yorkshire) Treasure Island (West coast of England) A Christmas Carol (London) Swallows and Amazons (Lake District) Black Beauty (Derbyshire)	<u>Another Country</u> 20,000 Leagues Under the Sea (Antarctic) The Jungle Book (India) Anne of Green Gables (Prince Edward Island, Canada) Little House in the Big Woods (Wisconsin, USA) The Call of the Wild (California, USA)
<u>North America</u> Anne of Green Gables (Prince Edward Island, Canada) Little House in the Big Woods (Wisconsin, USA) The Call of the Wild (California, USA)	<u>Fantasy</u> The Lion, the Witch and the Wardrobe (Narnia) The Hobbit (The Shire, Middle Earth)

The extracts in this book are ordered from easier to more difficult. Teachers may wish to use them in this order, select extracts linked to class topics/themes or choose those they think will most interest their class.

How to use this book

The content domain question types are organised in the order in which they appear in the National Curriculum but it is important that teachers think about the needs of their class and choose content domains accordingly. Teachers may wish to begin with more basic retrieval before moving on to more difficult content domains such as vocabulary or author's use of language. You will notice there are more vocabulary, retrieval and inference questions than the other content domains. This reflects the weighting of the question types in the KS2 Reading SATs papers and gives children more opportunities to practise these skills.

The extracts and questions have been designed to work well within a variety of teaching styles: whole class sessions, smaller teacher-led sessions or child-led groups. They may be used as a supported or independent task. The flexibility of this resource means it can be used in many different ways.

Each unit, consisting of an extract and eight question types, should be taught over a number of sessions, allowing the teacher time to really focus on the strategies needed to answer each question type.

Some of the extracts are intentionally difficult (much like the KS2 Reading SATs papers). However, the accompanying questions have been designed to guide children through the texts and help them to develop their comprehension and reading skills. All of the extracts have been trialled with my own Year 6 students. They commented that, at first, the texts seemed really difficult but once they worked through the questions, they understood what the story was about, had learned a lot of new vocabulary and gained insights into the texts.

The richness of these texts provides endless classroom opportunities. Rather than just reading and analysing the stand-alone extracts, teachers and their students may wish to bring a text to life through further exploration together.

Children may be inspired to write in a similar style or use the content of the extract to inspire their own compositions across a range of genres and purposes. The best writing often comes from meaningful classroom activities based on high-quality texts.

The classic extracts in this book lend themselves to a whole host of teaching activities. I would encourage teachers to use these texts as a springboard to jump off into further learning.

- Speaking and listening activities such as expressing opinions, questioning, description, persuasion and debate.
- Drama activities such as role-play, hot-seating, freeze-frame and characterisation.
- Historical research into the author, time period, technology, links to historical events, comparisons between time periods or a related educational visit (my 11-year-old daughter says anytime a local connection can be made to anything being studied at school, it's exciting and the learning is much more meaningful).

- Biographies of authors or historical characters.
- Geographical research into the setting location, study of geographical features (eg, islands, mountains, seas), and map drawing.
- ICT links such as computer animation, short films, book reviews, advertisements, and recording their own audio books complete with sound effects.
- Book to film comparisons.

Follow the children's lead. With some texts, they will be happy to read, practise the question types and move on while other texts will capture their imaginations and natural curiosity. Grab this and run with it! Be flexible, confident and enjoy the journey with them through the world of classic children's literature.

Reading Content Domain

Vocabulary

Give or explain the meaning of words in context.

The **Vocabulary** content domain is not only about the words children know but also the strategies they have for working out the meaning of words they don't know. Children must use the context of the surrounding sentence, paragraph or entire extract, to work out the meaning of the words. By thinking about what has been happening in the text so far and searching for clues, children are able to learn new words and expand their vocabulary. This content domain draws heavily on children's understanding of synonyms and their ability to use the "replacement method" in which they remove the word in question and replace it with each option in turn to find the best fit.

For example: **Swallows and Amazons**

In the question below, replace *"trooped"* with each option given to find the answer that best fits.

"*...and they all trooped out again...*"

Which word is closest in meaning to <u>trooped</u>?

	Tick **one**
walked	
crept	
stomped	
marched	

Retrieval

Retrieve and record information / identify key details from fiction and non-fiction.

The **Retrieval** content domain is about children being able to find key pieces of information in the text. Using keywords and a highlighting strategy will help children to make links between the keywords in the question and similar wording in the text. By scanning the text, they can spot the keywords, highlight them and find their answer. It is important to note that it may not be the exact wording from the questions in the text. Synonyms may be used.

For example: **Ann of Green Gables**

In the question below:

What is the mistake the stationmaster refers to?

The keywords are *"mistake"* and *"stationmaster"*.

Once the children find these words (or synonyms for them) in the text, they will be able to find their answer.

Summary

Summarise main ideas from more than one paragraph.

The *Summary* content domain is about children being able to sum up or condense what they have read. This may involve identifying the key points of a plot or coming up with an appropriate heading for a section of text. In these questions, more than one answer may be possible but children must choose the best or most appropriate answer.

> For example: **Black Beauty**
> In the question below, children are asked to identify the main idea/lesson of the entire extract. They need to choose the answer that provides the best overall meaning.
>
> Which is the main message of this extract?
>
> | | Tick **one** |
> | --- | --- |
> | Don't go out in a storm. | |
> | Humans are smarter than animals. | |
> | Humans should trust animals' instincts. | |
> | Always check before you cross a bridge. | |

Inference

Make inferences from the text/explain and justify inferences with evidence from the text.

The *Inference* content domain is about children being detectives and looking for clues in the text to support their answers. It is important for them to remember that whenever they make a point (or give an answer), they need to also provide a quote from or reference to the text that proves what they are saying.

> For example: **Anne of Green Gables**
> In the question below, children will find that the character of Anne is chatty, imaginative and brave. For each characteristic they identify, they must make a direct reference to the text to prove it.
>
> Look at the paragraph beginning, *"I suppose you are Mr. Matthew Cuthbert of Green Gables"*
> What impression do you get of Anne?

© Brilliant Publications Limited

Prediction

Predict what might happen from details stated and implied.

The **Prediction** content domain is about making logical or reasonable predictions about what might happen later in the story. Children should be able to back up their ideas with evidence from the text that has led them to believe in their predictions.

> For example: **Little House in the Big Woods**
>
> In the question below, children will need to put themselves in place of the character Laura and decide what they think she might do in the future. As well as ticking their answer, they must be able to justify their predictions by referring to how Laura felt in the extract.
>
> 'Based on what you have read, do you think Laura will want to help Ma with the milking again? Make a reasonable prediction with reference to the text.'
>
> | | Tick **one** |
> |-------|--------------|
> | yes | |
> | no | |
> | maybe | |

Text Meaning

Identify/explain how information/narrative content is related and contributes to meaning as a whole.

The **Text Meaning** content domain is about identifying the structural and language features of the extract and understanding the role of each part of the text. This includes explaining how certain parts of a text help to create or change the overall text meaning.

> For example: **Secret Garden**
> In the question below, children are required to match each feature of the text with an example.
>
> Draw lines to match each part of the story with the correct quotation from the text.
>
> - character — P'raps tha' art a young 'un, after all…
> - speech — "You showed me where the key was yesterday," she said,
> - action — …and he opened his beak and sang a loud, lovely trill, merely to show off.
> - dialect — …and suddenly a gust of wind swung aside some loose ivy trails…

Author's Use of Language

Identify/explain how meaning is enhanced through choice of words and phrases.

The *Author's Use of Language* content domain is about children recognising figurative language and descriptive phrases that contribute to the overall meaning of the text. Once children spot these features, they need to both understand what the features mean and identify the impact on the reader. There are various strategies children may use to answer these types of questions.

A) Mind Map method – Children identify the keyword in the question and place it at the centre of a mind map (spider diagram). They then write down everything they know about the word. Once they have thought through all of the possible meanings or associations of the word, they choose the most logical or best fit ideas to create their answer. If there is more than one word identified in the question, children should make sure they include an explanation or reference to each word in their answer.

For example: **The Secret Garden**

"Thick as the ivy hung, it nearly all was a loose and swinging curtain…"
What does "a loose and swinging curtain" suggest about the ivy?

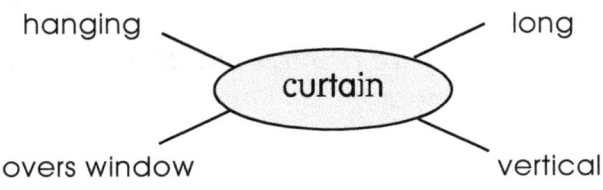

This tells us that the ivy is hanging down the wall and is probably covering it similarly to a curtain covering a window. Loose means the ends are not attached to the wall and it is moving in the wind.

B) Replacement method as described in the *Vocabulary* content domain.

C) Identify figurative language techniques (simile, metaphor, imagery, personification etc) and write about how the author is using that technique.

For example: **Little House in the Big Woods**

In the question below, the personification of the wind helps the reader to identify that Laura is frightened and worried that Pa may be lost in the night. The wind is crying just like Laura feels like crying.

"…the wind went crying as though it were lost in the dark and the cold."
How does this description of the wind help the reader understand Laura's feelings?

Compare and Contrast

Make comparisons within the text.

The **Comparison** content domain is about children identifying how characters, settings or events in an extract are similar or different to each other. It also requires children to identify how a character changes over the course of a story. When answering these questions, children must choose the most appropriate conjunction to link their ideas together as they build their answer.

To Show Similarity / Compare	To Show Difference / Contrast
similarly	but
also	however
in addition	on the other hand
in the same way	whereas
they are both…	while
likewise	yet
equally	unlike

> For example: **Little House in the Big Woods**
>
> In the question below, children are asked to identify how two animals are different. The use of contrasting conjunctions makes the answer very clear.
>
> Give two ways Sukey and the bear are different.
> 1. The bear has long, shaggy, black fur <u>but</u> Sukey has thin, short, brown fur.
> 2. The bear has little glimmering eyes <u>whereas</u> Sukey has large, gentle eyes.

Little House in the Big Woods

by Laura Ingalls Wilder

Then one day Pa said that spring was coming.

In the Big Woods the snow was beginning to thaw. Bits of it dropped from the branches of the trees and made little holes in the softening snowbanks below. At noon all the big icicles along the eaves of the little house quivered and sparkled in the sunshine, and drops of water hung trembling at their tips.

Pa said he must go to town to trade the furs of the wild animals he had been trapping all winter. So one evening he made a big bundle of them. There were so many furs that when they were packed tightly and tied together they made a bundle almost as big as Pa.

Very early one morning Pa strapped the bundle of furs on his shoulders, and started to walk to town. There were so many furs to carry that he could not take his gun.

Ma was worried, but Pa said that by starting before sun-up and walking very fast all day he could get home again before dark.

The nearest town was far away. Laura and Mary had never seen a town. They had never seen a store. They had never seen even two houses standing together. But they knew that in a town there were many houses, and a store full of candy and calico and other wonderful things—powder, and shot, and salt, and store sugar.

They knew that Pa would trade his furs to the storekeeper for beautiful things from town, and all day they were expecting the presents he would bring them. When the sun sank low above the treetops and no more drops fell from the tips of the icicles they began to watch eagerly for Pa.

The sun sank out of sight, the woods grew dark, and he did not come. Ma started supper and set the table, but he did not come. It was time to do the chores, and still he had not come.

Ma said that Laura might come with her while she milked the cow. Laura could carry the lantern.

So Laura put on her coat and Ma buttoned it up. And Laura put her hands into her red mittens that hung by a red yarn string around her neck, while Ma lighted the candle in the lantern.

Laura was proud to be helping Ma with the milking, and she carried the lantern very carefully. Its sides were of tin, with places cut in them for the candle-light to shine through.

When Laura walked behind Ma on the path to the barn, the little bits of candle-light from the lantern leaped all around her on the snow. The night was not yet quite dark. The woods were dark, but there was a gray light on the snowy path, and in the sky there were a few faint stars. The stars did not look as warm and bright as the little lights that came from the lantern.

Laura was surprised to see the dark shape of Sukey, the brown cow, standing at the barnyard gate. Ma was surprised, too.

It was too early in the spring for Sukey to be let out in the Big Woods to eat grass. She lived in the barn. But sometimes on warm days Pa left the door of her stall open so she could come into the barnyard. Now Ma and Laura saw her behind the bars, waiting for them.

Ma went up to the gate, and pushed against it to open it. But it did not open very far, because there was Sukey, standing against it. Ma said,

"Sukey, get over!" She reached across the gate and slapped Sukey's shoulder.

Just then one of the dancing little bits of light from the lantern jumped between the bars of the gate, and Laura saw long, shaggy, black fur, and two little, glittering eyes.

Sukey had thin, short, brown fur. Sukey had large, gentle eyes.

Ma said, "Laura, walk back to the house."

So Laura turned around and began to walk toward the house. Ma came behind her. When they had gone part way, Ma snatched her up, lantern and all, and ran. Ma ran with her into the house, and slammed the door. Then Laura said, "Ma, was it a bear?"

"Yes, Laura," Ma said. "It was a bear."

Laura began to cry. She hung on to Ma and sobbed, "Oh, will he eat Sukey?"

"No," Ma said, hugging her. "Sukey is safe in the barn. Think, Laura—all those big, heavy logs in the barn walls. And the door is heavy and solid, made to keep bears out. No, the bear cannot get in and eat Sukey."

Laura felt better then. "But he could have hurt us, couldn't he?" she asked.

"He didn't hurt us," Ma said. "You were a good girl, Laura, to do exactly as I told you, and to do it quickly, without asking why."

Ma was trembling, and she began to laugh a little. "To think," she said, "I've slapped a bear!"

Then she put supper on the table for Laura and Mary. Pa had not come yet. He didn't come. Laura and Mary were undressed, and they said their prayers and snuggled into the trundle bed.

Ma sat by the lamp, mending one of Pa's shirts. The house seemed cold and still and strange, without Pa.

Laura listened to the wind in the Big Woods. All around the house the wind went crying as though it were lost in the dark and the cold. The wind sounded frightened.

Ma finished mending the shirt. Laura saw her fold it slowly and carefully. She smoothed it with her hand. Then she did a thing she had never done before. She went to the door and pulled the leather latch-string through its hole in the door, so that nobody could get in from outside unless she lifted the latch. She came and took Carrie, all limp and sleeping, out of the big bed.

She saw that Laura and Mary were still awake, and she said to them: "Go to sleep, girls. Everything is all right. Pa will be here in the morning."

Then she went back to her rocking chair and sat there rocking gently and holding Baby Carrie in her arms.

She was sitting up late, waiting for Pa, and Laura and Mary meant to stay awake, too, till he came. But at last they went to sleep.

In the morning Pa was there. He had brought candy for Laura and Mary, and two pieces of pretty calico to make them each a dress. Mary's was a china-blue pattern on a white ground, and Laura's was dark red with little golden-brown dots on it. Ma had calico for a dress, too; it was brown, with a big, feathery white pattern all over it.

They were all happy because Pa had got such good prices for his furs that he could afford to get them such beautiful presents.

The tracks of the big bear were all around the barn, and there were marks of his claws on the walls. But Sukey and the horses were safe inside.

All that day the sun shone, the snow melted, and little streams of water ran from the icicles, which all the time grew thinner. Before the sun set that night, the bear tracks were only shapeless marks in the wet, soft snow.

Vocabulary — Little House in the Big Woods

1. Look at the beginning of the extract.
   Find and **copy one word** that is closest in meaning to <u>trembled</u>.
   _____

2. "*Pa said he must go to town to trade the furs of the wild animals...*".
   Which word is closest in meaning to <u>trade</u>?

	Tick **one**
sell	
exchange	
business	
buy	

3. Look at the paragraph beginning, "*So Laura turned around...*".
   Find and **copy two words** that show that Ma felt frightened.

   1. _____
   2. _____

4. **Find** and **copy a group of words** that tell you Ma wouldn't be able to sleep until Pa was home safely.
   _____
   _____
   _____

5. Based on what you have read, what is <u>calico</u>?
   _____
   _____

© Brilliant Publications Limited

Classic Children's Literature Years 5–6

Retrieval — Little House in the Big Woods

1. *"Then one day Pa said that spring was coming."*
   Find and **copy two pieces of evidence** that tell us spring is coming.

   1. _____
   2. _____

2. How long should it take for Pa to walk to town, trade the furs and walk home again?

   _____

3. What time of day is it when Laura and Mary begin watching for Pa to return?

	Tick **one**
dawn	
supper time	
sunset	
bedtime	

4. **Find** and **copy two phrases** that explain why Sukey is safe in the barn.

   1. _____
   2. _____

5. Using information from the text, put a tick in the correct box to show whether each statement is **true** or **false**.

	True	False
Pa went to town on horseback.		
Pa brought presents for Laura, Mary and Ma.		
The bear tried to get into the house.		
Sukey had escaped from the barn.		

Classic Children's Literature for KS2

Summary — Little House in the Big Woods

1. Which of the following would be the best title for this chapter of the book?

	Tick **one**
A Bear in the Barn	
Surprise in the Night	
Pa Goes to Town	
A Frightening Surprise	

2. Below are some summaries of different parts of this text. **Number them 1–6** to show the order in which they appear in the text. The first one has been done for you.

Pa prepared to go to town.	
Laura went to help Ma with the milking.	
The girls watched for Pa to come home.	
Ma slapped the bear.	
Ma started supper and did the chores.	
Spring was coming.	1

© Brilliant Publications Limited

Classic Children's Literature Years 5–6

Inference — Little House in the Big Woods

1. Where have the girls always lived? **Use evidence from the text** to support your answer.

   _____

   _____

2. Why do you think Laura felt proud to be helping Ma with the milking?

   _____

   _____

3. Why was Laura surprised to see the dark shape of Sukey standing by the barn gate?

   _____

   _____

4. Give **two reasons** why you think Laura began to cry once she and Ma returned to the house.

   1. _____

   2. _____

5. What does the action of pulling *"the leather latch-string through its hole in the door..."* tell you about how Ma is feeling?

   _____

   _____

6. What had the bear been trying to do during the night? Explain how you know.

   _____

   _____

Classic Children's Literature Years 5–6

Prediction   Little House in the Big Woods

1. Laura obeyed Ma at once and walked back to the house. What might have happened if Laura had fussed and disobeyed Ma?
Use evidence from the text to support your prediction.

_____
_____
_____
_____
_____
_____

2. Based on what you have read, do you think Laura will want to help Ma with the milking again?

	Tick **one**
yes	
no	
maybe	

Make a reasonable **prediction** with reference to the text.

_____
_____
_____
_____
_____
_____

© Brilliant Publications Limited   Classic Children's Literature Years 5–6

Text Meaning — Little House in the Big Woods

1. Draw lines to match each part of the story with the correct quotation from the text.

speech	Bits of it dropped from the branches of the trees…
character description	…Pa strapped the bundle of furs on his shoulders…
action	Ma was trembling…
setting	"You were a good girl, Laura, to do exactly as I told you…"

Classic Children's Literature Years 5–6 © Brilliant Publications Limited

Author's Use of Language — Little House in the Big Woods

1. *"Ma was trembling, and she began to laugh a little."*
What does the phrase *"began to laugh a little"* tell the reader about Ma's reaction to the bear?

	Tick **one**
She thought it was funny.	
She can't believe what has happened.	
She thinks it will be a funny story to tell Pa.	
She really likes bears.	

2. *"...the wind went crying as though it were lost in the dark and the cold."*
How does this description of the wind help the reader understand Laura's feelings?

_____
_____
_____
_____

3. **Find** and **copy a phrase** that gives the impression that it is not an ordinary evening for Ma and the girls.
_____

4. *"The house seemed cold, still and strange without Pa."*
What does this description suggest about the feeling in the house?

_____
_____
_____

© Brilliant Publications Limited

Classic Children's Literature Years 5–6

Compare and Contrast

Little House in the Big Woods

1. How is the light from the lantern different to the starlight?

   _____
   _____
   _____

2. a) Give **one** way Sukey and the bear are similar.

   1. _____

   b) Give **two** ways Sukey and the bear are different.

   1. _____

   2. _____

3. How do Laura's feelings change from the night to the morning?

   _____
   _____
   _____

The Lion, the Witch and the Wardrobe

by C. S. Lewis

But when next morning came there was a steady rain falling, so thick that when you looked out of the window you could see neither the mountains nor the woods nor even the stream in the garden.

"Of course it would be raining!" said Edmund. They had just finished their breakfast with the Professor and were upstairs in the room he had set apart for them—a long, low room with two windows looking out in one direction and two in another.

"Do stop grumbling, Ed," said Susan. "Ten to one it'll clear up in an hour or so. And in the meantime we're pretty well off. There's a wireless and lots of books."

"Not for me" said Peter. "I'm going to explore in the house."

Everyone agreed to this and that was how the adventures began. It was the sort of house that you never seem to come to the end of, and it was full of unexpected places. The first few doors they tried led only into spare bedrooms, as everyone had expected that they would; but soon they came to a very long room full of pictures and there they found a suit of armour; and after that was a room all hung with green, with a harp in one corner; and then came three steps down and five steps up, and then a kind of little upstairs hall and a door that led out on to a balcony, and then a whole series of rooms that led into each other and were lined with books—most of them very old books and some bigger than a Bible in a church. And shortly after that they looked into a room that was quite empty except for one big wardrobe; the sort that has a looking-glass in the door. There was nothing else in the room at all except a dead blue-bottle on the window-sill.

"Nothing there!" said Peter, and they all trooped out again—all except Lucy. She stayed behind because she thought it would be worth while trying the door of the wardrobe, even though she felt almost sure that it would be locked. To her surprise it opened quite easily, and two moth-balls dropped out.

Looking into the inside, she saw several coats hanging up—mostly long fur coats. There was nothing Lucy liked so much as the smell and feel of fur. She immediately stepped into the wardrobe and got in among the coats and rubbed her face against them, leaving the door open, of course, because she knew that it is very foolish to shut oneself into any wardrobe. Soon she went further in and found that there was a second row of coats hanging up behind the first one. It was almost quite dark in there and she kept her arms stretched out in front of her so as not to bump her face into the back of the wardrobe. She took a step further in—then two or three steps always expecting to feel woodwork against the tips of her fingers. But she could not feel it.

"This must be a simply enormous wardrobe!" thought Lucy, going still further in and pushing the soft folds of the coats aside to make room for her. Then she noticed that there was something crunching under her feet. "I wonder is that more mothballs?" she thought, stooping down to feel it with her hand. But instead of feeling the hard, smooth wood of the floor of the wardrobe, she felt something soft and powdery and extremely cold. "This is very queer," she said, and went on a step or two further.

Next moment she found that what was rubbing against her face and hands was no longer soft fur but something hard and rough and even prickly. "Why, it is just like branches of trees!" exclaimed Lucy. And then she saw that there was a light ahead of her; not a few inches away where the back of the wardrobe ought to have been, but a long way off. Something cold and soft was falling on her. A moment later she found that she was standing in the middle of a wood at night-time with snow under her feet and snowflakes falling through the air.

Lucy felt a little frightened, but she felt very inquisitive and excited as well. She looked back over her shoulder and there, between the dark tree trunks; she could still see the open doorway of the wardrobe and even catch a glimpse of the empty room from which she had set out. (She had, of course, left the door open, for she knew that it is a very silly thing to shut oneself into a wardrobe.) It seemed to be still daylight there. "I can always get back if anything goes wrong," thought Lucy. She began to walk forward, crunch-crunch over the snow and through the wood towards the other light. In about ten minutes she reached it and found it was a lamp-post. As she stood looking at it, wondering why there was a lamp-post in the middle of a wood and wondering what to do next, she heard a pitter patter of feet coming towards her. And soon after that a very strange person stepped out from among the trees into the light of the lamp-post.

He was only a little taller than Lucy herself and he carried over his head an umbrella, white with snow. From the waist upwards he was like a man, but his legs were shaped like a goat's (the hair on them was glossy black) and instead of feet he had goat's hoofs. He also had a tail, but Lucy did not notice this at first because it was neatly caught up over the arm that held the umbrella so as to keep it from trailing in the snow. He had a red woollen muffler round his neck and his skin was rather reddish too. He had a strange, but pleasant little face, with a short pointed beard and curly hair, and out of the hair there stuck two horns, one on each side of his forehead. One of his hands, as I have said, held the umbrella: in the other arm he carried several brown-paper parcels. What with the parcels and the snow it looked just as if he had been doing his Christmas shopping. He was a Faun. And when he saw Lucy he gave such a start of surprise that he dropped all his parcels.

Vocabulary — The Lion, the Witch and the Wardrobe

1. *"But when the next morning came..."*
Circle the correct options to complete the sentence below:

The rain was _____ and the children could see _____.

light	heavy
pitter-pattering	misty

the stream	the mountains
nothing	the mountains and the woods

---

2. *"There's a wireless and lots of books."*
Which word is closest in meaning to <u>wireless</u>?

	Tick **one**
telephone	
television	
radio	
newspaper	

---

3. *"...and they all trooped out again..."*
Which word is closest in meaning to <u>trooped</u>?

	Tick **one**
walked	
crept	
stomped	
marched	

---

4. Look at the paragraph beginning, *"Lucy felt a little frightened..."*.
Find and **copy one word** from this paragraph that is closest in meaning to <u>curious</u>.

_____

---

5. *"...a very strange person stepped out from among the trees..."*
What does <u>among the trees</u> mean in this sentence?

	Tick **one**
next to the trees	
behind the trees	
in the midst of the trees	
beyond the trees	

Classic Children's Literature Years 5–6

Retrieval — The Lion, the Witch and the Wardrobe

1. As the children explore the house, they discover many unexpected places.
Find and **copy five** examples of the unexpected things they find.

   1. _____
   2. _____
   3. _____
   4. _____
   5. _____

2. **Tick** the illustration which best matches the description of the Faun?

© Kate Heap and Brilliant Publications Limited

Classic Children's Literature for **KS2**

Retrieval — The Lion, the Witch and the Wardrobe

3. **Find** and **copy two reasons** why the Faun looked, "...*as if he had been doing his Christmas shopping.*"

   1. _____

   2. _____

4. At the beginning of the story, how many children are in the room together? **Circle one**.

   | 1 | 2 | 3 | 4 |

5. Using information from the text, put a tick in the correct box to show whether each statement is **true** or **false**.

	True	False
Lucy expected the wardrobe to be unlocked.		
There were three rows of coats in the wardrobe.		
Lucy could feel mothballs crunching underfoot.		
The sun shone brightly in the woods.		

Classic Children's Literature for KS2

Summary — The Lion, the Witch and the Wardrobe

1. Which of the following would be the best summary of the whole text?

	Tick **one**
Adventures in the House	
The Way into Narnia	
A New Friend	
Hide and Seek	

2. Below are some summaries of different paragraphs from this text.
   Number them 1–6 to show the order in which they appear in the text.
   The first one has been done for you.

Lucy walked to the lamp-post.	
The children decided to explore the house.	
Lucy spotted a Faun.	
The children found many unexpected places.	
The children had to play inside because of the rain.	1
Lucy decided to try the door of the wardrobe.	

3. Using information from the text, tick one box in each row to show whether each statement is **true** or **false**.

	True	False
Lucy is more curious than her siblings.		
The rainy day led them to new adventures.		
The wardrobe was another "unexpected place".		
It was a rainy day in the woods inside the wardrobe.		

Inference — The Lion, the Witch and the Wardrobe

1. Look at the first paragraph beginning, '"Nothing there!" said Peter...'.
What impression does this paragraph give you about Lucy's character?

_____
_____

2. Look at the paragraph beginning "Looking into the inside...".
Find and **copy a phrase** that demonstrates that Lucy thought she was in an ordinary wardrobe.

_____
_____

3. '"This must be a simply enormous wardrobe!" thought Lucy...'.
Why does Lucy think it "must be a simply enormous wardrobe"?

_____
_____

4. Lucy looks back to "catch a glimpse of the empty room from which she had set out." Why does she do this?

	Tick **one**
To check if anyone has followed her.	
To make sure she can find her way home.	
To use the light to help her see.	
To make sure she isn't trapped inside the wardrobe.	

5. Which of the four children appeals to you most? Why? Give evidence from the text to support your answer. Tick **one**.

☐ Edmund   ☐ Peter   ☐ Susan   ☐ Lucy

_____
_____

Classic Children's Literature Years 5–6

Prediction — The Lion, the Witch and the Wardrobe

1. Based on what you have read, predict how Lucy and the Faun will react to each other?
Use evidence from the text to support your prediction. Tick **one**.

☐ Run away

☐ Speak to each other

_____
_____
_____
_____
_____
_____
_____

© Brilliant Publications Limited

Classic Children's Literature Years 5–6

Text Meaning — The Lion, the Witch and the Wardrobe

1. Draw lines to match each part of the story with the correct quotation from the text.

character	From the waist upwards he was like a man, but his legs were shaped like a goat's...
rule	...crunch-crunch over the snow and...
onomatopoeia	...gave such a start of surprise that he dropped all his parcels.
action	...she knew that it is very foolish to shut oneself into any wardrobe.

Author's Use of Language

The Lion, the Witch and the Wardrobe

1. Susan says the children are *"pretty well off."*
Find and **copy two words or phrases** that suggest this.

   1. _____

   2. _____

2. "*...sort of house that you never seem to come to the end of...*"
What does this description suggest about the house?

   _____

   _____

3. "*– most of them very old books and some bigger than a Bible in a church.*"
What does ... some bigger than a Bible in a church tell you about the books the children found?

   _____

   _____

   _____

4. "*...she felt something soft and powdery and extremely cold.*"
What impression does the word powdery give of the snow on the ground?

   _____

   _____

5. "*...she heard a pitter patter of feet coming towards her.*"
What does this phrase suggest about the creature that comes towards Lucy?

   _____

   _____

© Brilliant Publications Limited

Classic Children's Literature Years 5–6

Compare and Contrast

The Lion, the Witch and the Wardrobe

1. Write **one** way the characters of Edmund and Susan are different.

   _____

   _____

2. As Lucy moves through the wardrobe, how does the sensation on her face change?

   _____

   _____

3. How are the characters of Lucy and the Faun similar?

   _____

   _____

Swallows and Amazons

by Arthur Ransome

At that moment something hit the saucepan with a loud ping, and ashes flew up out of the fire. A long arrow with a green feather stuck, quivering, among the embers.

The four explorers started to their feet.

"It's begun," said Titty.

Roger grabbed at the arrow and pulled it out of the fire.

Titty took it from him at once. "It may be poisoned," she said. "Don't touch the point of it."

"Listen," said Captain John.

They listened. There was not a sound to be heard but the quiet lapping of the water against the western shore of the island.

"It's him," said Titty. "He's winged his arrow with a feather from his green parrot."

"Listen," said Captain John again.

"Shut up, just for a minute," said Mate Susan.

There was the sharp crack of a dead stick breaking somewhere in the middle of the island.

"We must scout," said Captain John. "I'll take one end of the line, the mate the other. Titty and Roger go in the middle. Spread out. As soon as one of us sees him, the others close in to help."

They spread out across the island, and began to move forward. But they had not gone ten yards when John gave a shout.

"Swallow has gone," he shouted. He was on the left of the line, and as soon as he came out of the camping ground he saw the landing-place where he had left Swallow when he came back with the milk. No Swallow was there. The others ran together to the landing-place. There was not a sign of Swallow. She had simply disappeared.

"Spread out again. Spread out again," said John. "We'll comb the whole island. Keep a look-out, Mister Mate, from your shore. She can't have drifted away. He's taken her, but he's still on the island. We heard him."

"Roger and I pulled her right up," said Titty. "She couldn't have drifted off."

"Spread out again," said Captain John. "Then listen. Advance as soon as the mate blows her whistle. A hoot like an owl means all right. Three hoots means something's up. Blow as soon as you're ready, Mister Mate."

The mate crossed the island nearly to the western shore. She looked out through the trees. Not a sail was to be seen on the lake. Far away there was the smoke of the morning steamer, but that did not count. Roger and Titty, half a dozen yards apart, were in the middle of the island. Captain John moved a little way inland, but not so far that anyone could be between him and the shore without being seen. They listened. There was not a sound.

Then, over on the western side of the island, the mate blew her whistle.

The four began moving again through the trees and the undergrowth.

"Roger," called Titty, "have you got a weapon?"

"No," said Roger. "Have you?"

"I've got two sticks, pikes, I mean. You'd better have one."

She threw one of her sticks to Roger.

An owl hooted away to her left.

"That must be the captain," she said. She hooted back. Susan away on the right hooted in reply. Again they all listened. Then they moved forward again.

"Hullo," cried Roger, "some one's been here."

Titty ran to him. There was a round place where the grass and ferns were pressed flat as if someone had been lying there.

"He's left his knife," said Roger, holding up a big clasp knife that he had found in the grass.

Titty hooted like an owl three times.

The captain and the mate came running.

"He must be quite close to," said Titty.

"We've got his knife, anyway," said Roger.

Captain John bent down and felt the flattened grass with his hand.

"It's not warm," he said.

"Well, it wouldn't stay warm very long," said the mate.

"Spread out again and go on," said Captain John. "We mustn't let him get away with Swallow. He can't be far away, because we heard him. If he had taken Swallow to sea we should have seen her. He must have her here, somewhere, close along the shore."

At that moment there was a wild yell, "Hurrah, Hurrah." But the yelling did not come from in front of them. It came from behind them, from the direction of the camp.

"Come on," said Captain John, "keep together. Charge!"

The whole party rushed back through the trees towards the camp.

Just as they came to the edge of the clearing there was a shout, but they could see no one.

"Hands up! Halt!"

The voice came from immediately in front of them.

"Hands up!" it came again.

"Flat on your faces," cried Captain John, throwing himself on the ground.

Susan, Titty, and Roger were full length on the ground in a moment. An arrow passed harmlessly over their heads.

They looked at their own camp, and did not at first see what Captain John had seen. In the middle of the camp a tall stick was stuck in the ground with a black pirate flag blowing from the top of it. But there seemed to be nobody there. Then, inside their own tents, they saw two figures, kneeling, one with a bow ready to shoot, the other fitting an arrow.

Vocabulary — Swallows and Amazons

1. In the first paragraph, which word could best replace <u>quivering</u>? **Circle one**.

still	trembling
rocking	standing

2. Near the beginning of the extract, **find** and **copy one word** that shows the lake was calm that day.

   _____

3. "We must scout," said Captain John.
   The word <u>scout</u> suggests that the children will

	Tick **one**
have a meeting	
do reconnaissance	
protect the island	
go to camp	

4. "We'll comb the whole island."
   What does the word <u>comb</u> mean in this sentence?

   _____

5. "The whole party rushed back through the trees towards the camp."
   Find and copy a synonym for <u>rushed</u>.

   _____

6. The author of this text uses the word "said" in most of the characters' speech. Which word could replace "said" in the following sentences?
   "It may be poisoned," she said. "Don't touch the point of it." _____
   "Listen," said Captain John again. _____
   "Come on," said Captain John, "keep together. Charge!" _____

© Brilliant Publications Limited

Classic Children's Literature Years 5–6

41

Retrieval — Swallows and Amazons

1. After the arrow strikes, the children realise there is someone else on the island. List **three ways** they know this.

   1. _____
   2. _____
   3. _____

2. The children agree on a set of signals to help them communicate across the island. Put a tick in the correct box to show whether each statement is **true** or **false**.

	True	False
A blow on the whistle means danger.		
Three owl hoots mean they've found something.		
One owl hoot means everything's ok.		
Captain John will blow the whistle.		

3. *"Titty hooted like an owl three times."*

   Why did Titty give this signal?
   _____

4. Using information from the text, put a tick in the correct box to show whether each statement is **true** or **false**.

	True	False
There were many boats around the island.		
The grass was warm from where someone had been lying.		
Roger thinks The Swallow must be near, close to the shore.		
John spotted the invaders first.		

5. Why did it seem like there was no one at their camp?
   _____

Classic Children's Literature for KS2 © Kate Heap and Brilliant Publications Limited

Summary   Swallows and Amazons

1. Write a short summary about the character of John from this text.

_____
_____
_____
_____

2. Which of the following would be the best title for this text?

	Tick **one**
Stolen Swallow	
Who's There?	
Pirates Attack	
Making New Friends	

Explain your choice with reference to the text.

_____
_____
_____
_____

Inference   Swallows and Amazons

1. What were the children doing when the first arrow hit? Explain how you know with reference to the text.

_____
_____

2. Why do the children think they know who shot the arrow? Explain your answer with reference to the text.

_____
_____

3. What is The Swallow? **Give evidence** from the text to back up your answer.

_____
_____
_____

4. Why does the author say, "*Far away there was the smoke of the morning steamer, but that did not count*"?

_____
_____
_____

Classic Children's Literature Years 5–6   © Brilliant Publications Limited

Inference Swallows and Amazons

5. Think about the size of the island. Is it large or fairly small?

	Tick **one**
large	
small	

Explain how you know with reference to the text.

_____

_____

6. Think about your impression of the invaders on the island. Complete the table below with **one piece of evidence** to support each statement.

Impression	Evidence
The invaders are dangerous.	
The invaders are wild.	
The invaders are sneaky.	

Prediction   Swallows and Amazons

1. At the beginning of the extract, the day is calm and quiet. Do you think it will stay that way?

	Tick **one**
yes	
no	

Explain your prediction with reference to the text.

_____
_____
_____
_____

2. Do you think the children will give up their island to the invaders?

	Tick **one**
yes	
no	

Explain your prediction with reference to the text.

_____
_____
_____
_____

Classic Children's Literature Years 5–6   © Brilliant Publications Limited

Text Meaning — Swallows and Amazons

1. Draw lines to match each part of the story with the correct quotation from the text.

- clue
- speech
- setting
- action

- The whole party rushed back through the trees towards the camp.
- There was a round place where the grass and ferns were pressed flat as if someone had been lying there.
- There was not a sound to be heard but the quiet lapping of the water against the western shore of the island.
- "Hands up! Halt!"

2. Why do you think the author includes a lot of dialogue between the children in this text?

_____
_____
_____
_____

Author's Use of Language — Swallows and Amazons

1. At the beginning of this text, the author builds an atmosphere of suspense. **Find** and **copy three phrases** that help to build this atmosphere.

   1. _____
   2. _____
   3. _____

2. *"There was the sharp crack of a dead stick breaking somewhere in the middle of the island."*
In this line, which **two words** create a feeling of fear and mystery?

   1. _____
   2. _____

3. *"The four began moving again through the trees and the undergrowth."*
What impression does this sentence give you of the island?
_____
_____

Classic Children's Literature Years 5–6

Author's Use of Language — Swallows and Amazons

4. *"I've got two sticks, pikes, I mean. You'd better have one."*

Why does Titty change her word from <u>sticks</u> to <u>pikes</u>?

(pike: a historic infantry weapon with a pointed steel or iron head and a long wooden shaft)

_____
_____
_____
_____

5. Why does Captain John call out *"Charge!"* as the children move forward?

_____
_____
_____

6. What is the significance of the invaders' flag?

_____
_____
_____

Compare and Contrast — Swallows and Amazons

1. How do Roger and Titty react differently to the first arrow?

   _____
   _____
   _____

2. Compare the four children to the two invaders.
   a) How are they different?

   _____
   _____
   _____

   b) How are they similar?

   _____
   _____
   _____

The Call of the Wild

by Jack London

Buck did not read the newspapers, or he would have known that trouble was brewing, not alone for himself, but for every tide-water dog, strong of muscle and with warm, long hair, from Puget Sound to San Diego. Because men, groping in the Arctic darkness, had found a yellow metal, and because steamship and transportation companies were booming the find, thousands of men were rushing into the Northland. These men wanted dogs, and the dogs they wanted were heavy dogs, with strong muscles by which to toil, and furry coats to protect them from the frost.

Buck lived at a big house in the sun-kissed Santa Clara Valley. Judge Miller's place, it was called. It stood back from the road, half hidden among the trees, through which glimpses could be caught of the wide cool veranda that ran around its four sides. The house was approached by gravelled driveways which wound about through wide-spreading lawns and under the interlacing boughs of tall poplars. At the rear things were on even a more spacious scale than at the front. There were great stables, where a dozen grooms and boys held forth, rows of vine-clad servants' cottages, an endless and orderly array of outhouses, long grape arbours, green pastures, orchards, and berry patches. Then there was the pumping plant for the artesian well, and the big cement tank where Judge Miller's boys took their morning plunge and kept cool in the hot afternoon.

And over this great demesne Buck ruled. Here he was born, and here he had lived the four years of his life. It was true, there were other dogs, There could not but be other dogs on so vast a place, but they did not count. They came and went, resided in the populous kennels, or lived obscurely in the recesses of the house after the fashion of Toots, the Japanese pug, or Ysabel, the Mexican hairless, – strange creatures that rarely put nose out of doors or set foot to ground. On the other hand, there were the fox terriers, a score of them at least, who yelped fearful promises at Toots and Ysabel looking out of the windows at them and protected by a legion of housemaids armed with brooms and mops.

But Buck was neither house-dog nor kennel-dog. The whole realm was his. He plunged into the swimming tank or went hunting with the Judge's sons; he escorted Mollie and Alice, the Judge's daughters, on long twilight or early morning rambles; on wintry nights he lay at the Judge's feet before the roaring library fire; he carried the Judge's grandsons on his back, or rolled them in the grass, and guarded their footsteps through wild adventures down to the fountain in the stable yard, and even beyond, where the paddocks were, and the berry patches. Among the terriers he stalked imperiously, and Toots and Ysabel he utterly ignored, for he was king,—king over all creeping, crawling, flying things of Judge Miller's place, humans included.

His father, Elmo, a huge St. Bernard, had been the Judge's inseparable companion, and Buck bid fair to follow in the way of his father. He was not so large,—he weighed only one hundred and forty pounds,—for his mother, Shep, had been a Scotch shepherd dog. Nevertheless, one hundred and forty pounds, to which was added the dignity that comes of good living and universal respect, enabled him to carry himself in right royal fashion. During the four years since his puppyhood he had lived the life of a sated aristocrat; he had a fine pride in himself, was even a trifle egotistical, as country gentlemen sometimes become because of their insular situation. But he had saved himself by not becoming a mere pampered house-dog. Hunting and kindred outdoor delights had kept down the fat and hardened his muscles; and to him, as to the cold-tubbing races, the love of water had been a tonic and a health preserver.

And this was the manner of dog Buck was in the fall of 1897, when the Klondike strike dragged men from all the world into the frozen North.

Vocabulary   The Call of the Wild

1. Where does Buck live when the Klondike strike begins?

	Tick **one**.
Alaska	
California	
Arctic	
Japan	

2. What was the <u>yellow metal</u> found by the men in the Arctic?
_____

3. In the first paragraph, **find** and **copy a synonym** for <u>Arctic</u>.
_____

4. *"And over this great demesne Buck ruled."*
Which word could best replace <u>demesne</u> in this sentence? **Circle one**.

land	farm
house	garden

5. In the paragraph beginning, *"His father, Elmo..."*, **find** and **copy one word** that shows Buck was vain.
_____

6. *"...he had a fine pride in himself, was even a trifle egotistical, as country gentlemen sometimes become because of their insular situation."*
Which word could best replace <u>insular</u> in this sentence? **Circle one**.

peaceful	lonely
open-minded	inward-looking

Retrieval — The Call of the Wild

1. In the first paragraph, what type of dog do the men want?

    1. _____
    2. _____
    3. _____

2. For what purpose did the family use the big cement tank?

    _____

3. Name the two other dogs who lived in the house with Buck.

    1. _____
    2. _____

4. What role did Buck play with the Judge's grandsons?

    _____

5. Using information from the text, put a **tick** in the correct box to show whether each statement is **true** or **false**.

	True	False
Many men were travelling south.		
Buck lived in a kennel.		
Buck had lived at Judge Miller's place all his life.		
Buck liked to walk with Judge Miller's daughters, Mollie and Sarah.		

Classic Children's Literature for KS2

© Kate Heap and Brilliant Publications Limited

Summary: The Call of the Wild

1. *"But Buck was neither house-dog nor kennel-dog."*
What type of dog is Buck if he is neither a house-dog nor a kennel-dog? Explain your answer with reference to the text.

_____

_____

_____

2. Which of the following would be the best summary of the whole text?

	Tick **one**
King Over All	
A New Adventure	
Moving North	
House Dogs vs Kennel Dogs	

Inference The Call of the Wild

1. *"Buck did not read the newspapers, or he would have known that trouble was brewing..."*

Why didn't Buck read the newspapers?

_____

2. *"...or he would have known that trouble was brewing..."*

What does this line suggest about Buck's life?

	Tick **one**
Buck is going to learn to read.	
Buck gets lost.	
Buck's life is about to change.	
Buck is going to be in trouble.	

3. Look at the paragraph beginning, *"Buck lived in a big house in the sun-kissed Santa Clara Valley."*

What impression do you get of the house and grounds? **Give evidence** to support your answers.

Impression	Evidence

4. Look at the paragraph beginning, *"And over this great demesne..."*.

Why does Buck think the other dogs <u>did not count</u>? Give evidence from the text to support your answer.

_____

_____

Classic Children's Literature Years 5–6   © Brilliant Publications Limited

Inference — The Call of the Wild

5. The text suggests that Buck was well-loved by the Judge's family. **Find** and **copy three** pieces of evidence to support this statement.

   1. _____
   2. _____
   3. _____

6. Why were "...*men from all the world...*" going North?
   _____
   _____
   _____

Prediction — The Call of the Wild

1. Why do you think the men want dogs in the Arctic?

   _____
   _____
   _____

2. What do you think will happen to Buck? **Use evidence** from the text to support your answer.

   _____
   _____
   _____
   _____
   _____
   _____
   _____
   _____

Text Meaning — The Call of the Wild

1. Draw lines to match each part of the story with the correct quotation from the text.

   character — At the rear things were on even a more spacious scale than at the front.

   warning — ...plunged into the swimming tank...

   setting — Buck was neither a house-dog nor a kennel-dog.

   action — ...trouble was brewing...

2. Where would you expect to find this extract in the full book of The Call of the Wild?

	Tick **one**
Near the beginning	
In the middle	
Near the end	

   Why?

   _____
   _____
   _____
   _____

Author's Use of Language — The Call of the Wild

1. Toots and Ysabel are "*...protected by a legion of housemaids armed with brooms and mops.*"
   What does this phrase suggest about the housemaids?
   _____
   _____
   _____

2. In the fourth paragraph it says, "*...for he was king...*".
   Using the whole text, **find** and **copy five words or phrases** that emphasise this fact.

   1. _____   4. _____
   2. _____   5. _____
   3. _____

3. "*...as country gentlemen sometimes become because of their insular situation.*"
   What does the phrase <u>country gentlemen</u> suggest about Buck?
   _____
   _____

4. The reader does not find out the year in which the story takes place until the end of this extract. **Find** and **copy two clues** the author gives that suggest the story takes place during the Victorian Era.

   1. _____
   2. _____

5. "*Hunting and kindred outdoor delights...*"
   What impression does the word <u>kindred</u> give of Buck's relationship with the humans?
   _____
   _____

Classic Children's Literature Years 5–6

Compare and Contrast — The Call of the Wild

1. How does the Santa Clara Valley, where Buck lives, compare to the Arctic?
   _____
   _____

2. Write **one** way the fox terriers and the house-dogs, Toots and Ysabel, are different.
   _____
   _____

3. How do Buck and the house-dogs react differently to the outdoors?
   _____
   _____

4. a) How is Buck's relationship with the Judge similar to his relationship with the Judge's grandsons?
   _____
   _____

   b) How is it different?
   _____
   _____

5. a) How is Buck similar to his father?
   _____
   _____

   b) How is Buck different to his father?
   _____
   _____

© Brilliant Publications Limited

Classic Children's Literature Years 5–6

The Hobbit

by J. R. R. Tolkien

In a hole in the ground there lived a hobbit. Not a nasty, dirty, wet hole, filled with the ends of worms and an oozy smell, nor yet a dry, bare, sandy hole with nothing in it to sit down on or to eat: it was a hobbit-hole, and that means comfort.

It had a perfectly round door like a porthole, painted green, with a shiny yellow brass knob in the exact middle. The door opened on to a tube-shaped hall like a tunnel: a very comfortable tunnel without smoke, with panelled walls, and floors tiled and carpeted, provided with polished chairs, and lots and lots of pegs for hats and coats—the hobbit was fond of visitors. The tunnel wound on and on, going fairly but not quite straight into the side of the hill—The Hill, as all the people for many miles round called it—and many little round doors opened out of it, first on one side and then on another. No going upstairs for the hobbit: bedrooms, bathrooms, cellars, pantries (lots of these), wardrobes (he had whole rooms devoted to clothes), kitchens, dining-rooms, all were on the same floor, and indeed on the same passage. The best rooms were all on the left-hand side (going in), for these were the only ones to have windows, deep-set round windows looking over his garden and meadows beyond, sloping down to the river.

This hobbit was a very well-to-do hobbit, and his name was Baggins. The Bagginses had lived in the neighbourhood of The Hill for time out of mind, and people considered them very respectable, not only because most of them were rich, but also because they never had any adventures or did anything unexpected: you could tell what a Baggins would say on any question without the bother of asking him. This is a story of how a Baggins had an adventure, found himself doing and saying things altogether unexpected. He may have lost the neighbours' respect, but he gained— well, you will see whether he gained anything in the end.

The mother of our particular hobbit... what is a hobbit? I suppose hobbits need some description nowadays, since they have become rare and shy of the Big People, as they call us. They are (or were) a little people, about half our height, and smaller than the bearded Dwarves. Hobbits have no beards. There is little or no magic about them, except the ordinary everyday sort which helps them to disappear quietly and quickly when large stupid folk like you and me come blundering along, making a noise like elephants which they can hear a mile off. They are inclined to be fat in the stomach; they dress in bright colours (chiefly green and yellow); wear no shoes, because their feet grow natural leathery soles and thick warm brown hair like the stuff on their heads (which is curly); have long clever brown fingers, good-natured faces, and laugh deep fruity laughs (especially after dinner, which they have twice a day when they can get it). Now you know enough to go on with.

Vocabulary — The Hobbit

1. a) **Find** and **copy one** simile used to describe one feature of Baggins' house.
   _____

   b) To what type of object does this simile compare the hobbit-hole?
   _____

2. *"The Bagginses had lived in the neighbourhood of The Hill for time out of mind..."*
   Which phrase is closest in meaning to <u>time out of mind</u>?

	Tick **one**
many years	
since the hobbit was young	
a short while	
for longer than anyone can remember	

3. **Circle** the **two words** that best describe how hobbits are presented in the third paragraph.

kind	rich
predictable	safe

4. *"...when large stupid folk like you and me come blundering along..."*
   Which word is closest in meaning to <u>blundering</u>?

	Tick **one**
gracefully	
stomping	
striding	
clumsy	

Retrieval The Hobbit

1. Tick the illustration which best matches the description of the hobbit-hole door?

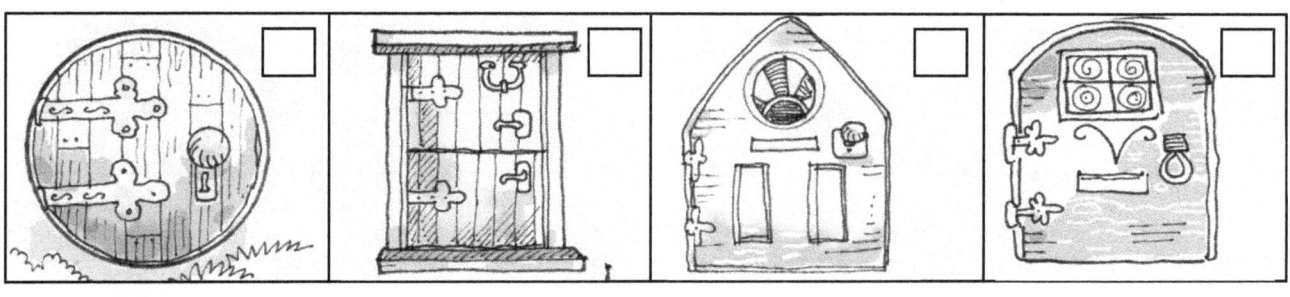

2. Why are we called *"Big People"*?
   _____
   _____

3. What sort of magic do hobbits have?
   _____
   _____

4. What is unusual about a hobbit's feet?
   _____
   _____

5. Using information from the text, put a **tick** in the correct box to show whether each statement is **true** or **false**.

	True	False
Hobbits are not magical.		
Hobbits have good hearing.		
Hobbits enjoy eating.		
There are many hobbits in existence.		

© Kate Heap and Brilliant Publications Limited

Classic Children's Literature for KS2

Summary — The Hobbit

1. Write **one to two sentences** to summarise the description of the hobbit's home in the second paragraph.

   _____
   _____
   _____
   _____

2. **Tick** the best heading for the third paragraph.

	Tick **one**
The Life of a Hobbit	
Changing his Ways	
An Unexpected Adventure	
A Different Sort of Hobbit	

3. Using information from the text, **tick one box** in each row to show whether each statement is **true** or **false**.

	True	False
He is just like all other hobbits.		
He always knew he'd have an adventure.		
Hobbits are unusual creatures.		

Classic Children's Literature Years 5–6 © Brilliant Publications Limited

Inference   The Hobbit

1. Look at the paragraph, beginning *"This hobbit was a very well-to-do hobbit..."*. Complete the table below with a piece of evidence from the story to support each statement.

Statement	Evidence
Hobbits lead a quiet life.	
Hobbits get on with their neighbours.	

2. Look at the paragraph beginning *"The mother of our particular hobbit..."*.
What impressions do you get of the hobbit's personality? Give evidence from the text to support your answer.

_____
_____
_____
_____

3. Based on the text, what does the author think about humans? **Give evidence** from the text to support your answer.

_____
_____
_____
_____

© Brilliant Publications Limited

Classic Children's Literature Years 5–6

Inference — The Hobbit

4. What does the phrase *"long clever brown fingers"* tell you about hobbits?

_____

_____

_____

_____

5. Put a **tick** in the correct box to show whether each of the following statements is a **fact** or **opinion**.

	Fact	Opinion
The best rooms were all on the left-hand side.		
He may have lost the neighbours' respect.		
Hobbits enjoy their food.		
The hobbit lives in a comfortable hole.		

Prediction — The Hobbit

1. *"He may have lost the neighbours' respect, but he gained — well, you will see whether he gained anything in the end."*

What do you think the hobbit will gain during his adventure? Give **two** answers with reasons for each of your answers.

1. _____
   _____
   _____
   _____

2. _____
   _____
   _____
   _____

Text Meaning — The Hobbit

1. Where would you expect to find this extract in the full book of The Hobbit?

	Tick **one**
Near the beginning	
In the middle	
Near the end	

Why?
_____
_____
_____
_____

2. In the fourth paragraph, the author was about to describe the hobbit's mother. Why did he stop?
_____
_____
_____
_____

Classic Children's Literature Years 5–6

Author's Use of Language — The Hobbit

1. The author creates an atmosphere of comfort. **Find** and **copy five phrases** that contribute to this.

   1. _____
   2. _____
   3. _____
   4. _____
   5. _____

2. Why do you think the author doesn't tell the reader what the hobbit gained on his adventure?

   _____
   _____
   _____

3. At the beginning of the extract, the author describes two types of hole. Neither sounds appealing. **Find** and **copy two words or phrases** for each hole used to achieve this effect.

Hole 1	Hole 2

Compare and Contrast — The Hobbit

1. How will this hobbit's life differ to that of his ancestors?
   _____
   _____
   _____
   _____
   _____

2. How do hobbits compare to dwarves?
   _____
   _____
   _____

3. To what does the author compare humans?
   _____
   _____
   _____

Anne of Green Gables

by Lucy Maud Montgomery

When he reached Bright River there was no sign of any train; he thought he was too early, so he tied his horse in the yard of the small Bright River hotel and went over to the station house. The long platform was almost deserted; the only living creature in sight being a girl who was sitting on a pile of shingles at the extreme end. Matthew, barely noting that it WAS a girl, sidled past her as quickly as possible without looking at her. Had he looked he could hardly have failed to notice the tense rigidity and expectation of her attitude and expression. She was sitting there waiting for something or somebody and, since sitting and waiting was the only thing to do just then, she sat and waited with all her might and main.

Matthew encountered the stationmaster locking up the ticket office preparatory to going home for supper, and asked him if the five-thirty train would soon be along.

"The five-thirty train has been in and gone half an hour ago," answered that brisk official. "But there was a passenger dropped off for you—a little girl. She's sitting out there on the shingles. I asked her to go into the ladies' waiting room, but she informed me gravely that she preferred to stay outside. 'There was more scope for imagination,' she said. She's a case, I should say."

"I'm not expecting a girl," said Matthew blankly. "It's a boy I've come for. He should be here. Mrs. Alexander Spencer was to bring him over from Nova Scotia for me."

The stationmaster whistled.

"Guess there's some mistake," he said. "Mrs. Spencer came off the train with that girl and gave her into my charge. Said you and your sister were adopting her from an orphan asylum and that you would be along for her presently. That's all I know about it—and I haven't got any more orphans concealed hereabouts."

"I don't understand," said Matthew helplessly, wishing that Marilla was at hand to cope with the situation.

"Well, you'd better question the girl," said the stationmaster carelessly. "I dare say she'll be able to explain—she's got a tongue of her own, that's certain. Maybe they were out of boys of the brand you wanted."

He walked jauntily away, being hungry, and the unfortunate Matthew was left to do that which was harder for him than bearding a lion in its den—walk up to a girl—a strange girl—an orphan girl—and demand of her why she wasn't a boy. Matthew groaned in spirit as he turned about and shuffled gently down the platform towards her.

She had been watching him ever since he had passed her and she had her eyes on him now. Matthew was not looking at her and would not have seen what she was really like if he had been, but an ordinary observer would have seen this: A child of about eleven, garbed in a very short, very tight, very ugly dress of yellowish-gray wincey. She wore a faded brown sailor hat and beneath the hat, extending down her back, were two braids of very thick, decidedly red hair. Her face was small, white and thin, also much freckled; her mouth was large and so were her eyes, which looked green in some lights and moods and gray in others.

So far, the ordinary observer; an extraordinary observer might have seen that the chin was very pointed and pronounced; that the big eyes were full of spirit and vivacity; that the mouth was sweet-lipped and expressive; that the forehead was broad and full; in short, our discerning extraordinary observer might have concluded that no commonplace soul inhabited the body of this stray woman-child of whom shy Matthew Cuthbert was so ludicrously afraid.

Matthew, however, was spared the ordeal of speaking first, for as soon as she concluded that he was coming to her she stood up, grasping with one thin brown hand the handle of a shabby, old-fashioned carpet-bag; the other she held out to him.

"I suppose you are Mr Matthew Cuthbert of Green Gables?" she said in a peculiarly clear, sweet voice. "I'm very glad to see you. I was beginning to be afraid you weren't coming for me and I was imagining all the things that might have happened to prevent you. I had made up my mind that if you didn't come for me to-night I'd go down the track to that big wild cherry-tree at the bend, and climb up into it to stay all night. I wouldn't be a bit afraid, and it would be lovely to sleep in a wild cherry-tree all white with bloom in the moonshine, don't you think? You could imagine you were dwelling in marble halls, couldn't you? And I was quite sure you would come for me in the morning, if you didn't to-night."

Matthew had taken the scrawny little hand awkwardly in his; then and there he decided what to do. He could not tell this child with the glowing eyes that there had been a mistake; he would take her home and let Marilla do that. She couldn't be left at Bright River anyhow, no matter what mistake had been made, so all questions and explanations might as well be deferred until he was safely back at Green Gables.

Vocabulary — Anne of Green Gables

1. "...the big eyes were full of spirit and vivacity..."
Which word is closest in meaning to vivacity?

	Tick **one**
quiet	
power	
energy	
strength	

2. "The long platform was almost deserted..."
What does almost deserted mean?

_____
_____

3. Look at the paragraph beginning, "The five thirty train...".
Find and **copy one word** from this paragraph that is closest in meaning to seriously.

_____

4. **Find** and **copy a group of words** that tells you that Anne had strong opinions and could speak for herself.

_____

5. "Matthew groaned in spirit as he turned about and shuffled gently down the platform towards her."
Circle the correct option to complete each sentence below:

Matthew felt _____ as he _____ towards Anne.

disappointed	anxious
dread	hopeless

strolled	moved slowly
rushed	tripped

Classic Children's Literature Years 5–6

Retrieval — Anne of Green Gables

1. Why did Matthew think he was too early to meet the train?
   _____

2. Look at the first paragraph. **Find** and **copy two words** or phrases that tell how Anne was waiting for Matthew.
   _____
   _____

3. What is the mistake the stationmaster refers to?
   _____

4. Write down **three things** you are told about Anne's appearance.
   1. _____
   2. _____
   3. _____

5. Using information from the text, put a **tick** in the correct box to show whether each statement is **true** or **false**.

	True	False
Matthew paid a great deal of attention to the child waiting on the platform.		
Mrs. Spencer told the stationmaster that Matthew and Marilla were expecting a girl from the orphan asylum.		
Matthew spoke first when he approached Anne.		
Matthew told Anne there had been a mistake.		

© Kate Heap and Brilliant Publications Limited

Classic Children's Literature for KS2

Summary   Anne of Green Gables

1. Below are some summaries of different paragraphs from this text. **Number them 1–6** to show the order in which they appear in the text. The first one has been done for you.

Matthew discovers there's been a mistake.	
Matthew decides to take Anne home with him.	
Matthew approaches the girl.	
Matthew arrives at Bright River train station.	1
Anne tells Matthew all about her plan to sleep in the wild cherry tree.	
The stationmaster tells Matthew the 5:30 train has already been and there was a passenger dropped off for him.	

2. Which of the following would be the best summary of the whole text?

	Tick **one**
New Friends	
Matthew's Mistake	
Unexpected Arrival	
The Train is Early	

3. Using information from the text, tick one box in each row to show whether each statement is **true** or **false**.

	True	False
Matthew is happy to see Anne.		
Matthew is a confident man.		
Anne is a chatterbox.		
Anne is an ordinary sort of child.		

Classic Children's Literature Years 5–6   © Brilliant Publications Limited

Inference — Anne of Green Gables

1. This part of the story takes place in the early evening. List **three clues** that tell you this.

   1. _____
   2. _____
   3. _____

2. Look at the first paragraph beginning, "When he reached Bright River...".
"Matthew, barely noticing that it WAS a girl, sidled past her as quickly as possible without looking at her."
Why does Matthew do this?

	Tick **one**
He didn't notice she was there.	
He doesn't want to trip over her bag.	
He is an introverted person who doesn't like speaking to others.	
He doesn't like girls.	

3. '"I don't understand," said Matthew helplessly, wishing that Marilla was at hand to cope with the situation.'
What does this sentence tell you about Marilla?
_____
_____

4. Look at the paragraph beginning, "She had been watching him...". What does this tell you about Anne's wealth? Is she rich or poor? Explain your answer with text references.
_____
_____
_____

5. Look at the paragraph beginning, "I suppose you are Mr Matthew Cuthbert of Green Gables?". What impression do you get of Anne?
_____
_____

© Brilliant Publications Limited

Classic Children's Literature Years 5–6

Prediction — Anne of Green Gables

1. Based on what you have read, what do you think will happen when Matthew takes Anne home to Marilla?
Use evidence from the text to support your prediction.

_____
_____
_____
_____
_____
_____

2. Do you think Anne and Matthew will become friends?

	Tick **one**
yes	
no	
maybe	

Explain your prediction with reference to the text.

_____
_____
_____
_____
_____
_____

Classic Children's Literature Years 5–6

Text Meaning — Anne of Green Gables

1. Draw lines to match each part of the story with the correct quotation from the text.

setting	He walked jauntily away, being hungry…
character	Mrs Spencer came off the train with that girl…
action	…answered that brisk official.
past event	The long platform was almost deserted.

Author's Use of Language — Anne of Green Gables

1. *"... but she informed me gravely that she preferred to stay outside. 'There was more scope for the imagination,' she said."*
What does Anne mean by <u>scope for the imagination</u>?
_____
_____
_____
_____

2. Why does Anne think it would be *"lovely to sleep in a wild cherry-tree all white with bloom in the moonshine"*?
_____
_____
_____
_____

3. *"Matthew was left to do that which was harder for him than bearding a lion in its den..."*
What does this description suggest about Matthew?
_____
_____
_____
_____

4. *"...no commonplace soul inhabited the body of this stray woman-child..."*
Give **two** impressions this gives you of Anne.
   1. _____
   2. _____

Classic Children's Literature Years 5–6

Compare and Contrast — Anne of Green Gables

1. Write **one** way the characters of Anne and Matthew are different.
   _____
   _____

2. Anne compares the cherry tree to marble halls. List **two** ways they are similar.
   _____
   _____
   _____
   _____

Black Beauty

by Anna Sewell

One day late in the autumn my master had a long journey to go on business. I was put into the dog-cart, and John went with his master. I always liked to go in the dog-cart, it was so light and the high wheels ran along so pleasantly. There had been a great deal of rain, and now the wind was very high and blew the dry leaves across the road in a shower. We went along merrily till we came to the toll-bar and the low wooden bridge. The river banks were rather high, and the bridge, instead of rising, went across just level, so that in the middle, if the river was full, the water would be nearly up to the woodwork and planks; but as there were good substantial rails on each side, people did not mind it.

The man at the gate said the river was rising fast, and he feared it would be a bad night. Many of the meadows were under water, and in one low part of the road the water was halfway up to my knees; the bottom was good, and master drove gently, so it was no matter.

When we got to the town of course I had a good bait, but as the master's business engaged him a long time we did not start for home till rather late in the afternoon. The wind was then much higher, and I heard the master say to John that he had never been out in such a storm; and so I thought, as we went along the skirts of a wood, where the great branches were swaying about like twigs, and the rushing sound was terrible.

"I wish we were well out of this wood," said my master.

"Yes, sir," said John, "it would be rather awkward if one of these branches came down upon us."

The words were scarcely out of his mouth when there was a groan, and a crack, and a splitting sound, and tearing, crashing down among the other trees came an oak, torn up by the roots, and it fell right across the road just before us. I will never say I was not frightened, for I was. I stopped still, and I believe I trembled; of course I did not turn round or run away; I was not brought up to that. John jumped out and was in a moment at my head.

"That was a very near touch," said my master. "What's to be done now?"
"Well, sir, we can't drive over that tree, nor yet get round it; there will be nothing for it, but to go back to the four crossways, and that will be a good six miles before we get round to the wooden bridge again; it will make us late, but the horse is fresh."

So back we went and round by the crossroads, but by the time we got to the bridge it was very nearly dark; we could just see that the water was over the middle of it; but as that happened sometimes when the floods were out, master did not stop. We were going along at a good pace, but the moment my feet touched the first part of the bridge I felt sure there was something wrong. I dare not go forward, and I made a dead stop. "Go on, Beauty," said my master, and he gave me a touch with the whip, but I dare not stir; he gave me a sharp cut; I jumped, but I dare not go forward.

"There's something wrong, sir," said John, and he sprang out of the dog-cart and came to my head and looked all about. He tried to lead me forward. "Come on, Beauty, what's the matter?" Of course I could not tell him, but I knew very well that the bridge was not safe.

Just then the man at the toll-gate on the other side ran out of the house, tossing a torch about like one mad.

"Hoy, hoy, hoy! halloo! stop!" he cried.

"What's the matter?" shouted my master.
"The bridge is broken in the middle, and part of it is carried away; if you come on you'll be into the river."

"Thank God!" said my master. "You Beauty!" said John, and took the bridle and gently turned me round to the right-hand road by the river side. The sun had set some time; the wind seemed to have lulled off after that furious blast which tore up the tree. It grew darker and darker, stiller and stiller. I trotted quietly along, the wheels hardly making a sound on the soft road. For a good while neither master nor John spoke, and then master began in a serious voice. I could not understand much of what they said, but I found they thought, if I had gone on as the master wanted me, most likely the bridge would have given way under us, and horse, chaise, master, and man would have fallen into the river; and as the current was flowing very strongly, and there was no light and no help at hand, it was more than likely we should all have been drowned. Master said, God had given men reason, by which they could find out things for themselves; but he had given animals knowledge which did not depend on reason, and which was much more prompt and perfect in its way, and by which they had often saved the lives of men. John had many stories to tell of dogs and horses, and the wonderful things they had done; he thought people did not value their animals half enough nor make friends of them as they ought to do. I am sure he makes friends of them if ever a man did.

At last we came to the park gates and found the gardener looking out for us. He said that mistress had been in a dreadful way ever since dark, fearing some accident had happened, and that she had sent James off on Justice, the roan cob, toward the wooden bridge to make inquiry after us.

We saw a light at the hall-door and at the upper windows, and as we came up mistress ran out, saying, "Are you really safe, my dear? Oh! I have been so anxious, fancying all sorts of things. Have you had no accident?"

"No, my dear; but if your Black Beauty had not been wiser than we were we should all have been carried down the river at the wooden bridge." I heard no more, as they went into the house, and John took me to the stable. Oh, what a good supper he gave me that night, a good bran mash and some crushed beans with my oats, and such a thick bed of straw! And I was glad of it, for I was tired.

Vocabulary — Black Beauty

1. *"We went along merrily till we came to the toll-bar..."*
Which word is closest in meaning to merrily?

	Tick **one**
quickly	
excitedly	
slowly	
happily	

2. *"...but as there were good substantial rails on each side..."*
What is the author saying about the rails?
_____

3. **Find** and **copy one word** that means it would be difficult if a tree branch fell.
_____

4. *"The sun had set some time; the wind seemed to have lulled off after that furious blast which tore up the tree."*
Which word is closest in meaning to lulled off?

Circle **one**	
continued	stopped
calmed	increased

5. *"...it will make us late, but the horse is fresh."*
Choose the best description of the horse:

	Tick **one**
The horse is new.	
The horse is well rested.	
The horse is young.	
The horse is healthy.	

Retrieval   Black Beauty

1. Look at the second paragraph beginning, *"The man at the gate...".*
Find and **copy three** signs of flooding in this paragraph.

   1. _____
   2. _____
   3. _____

2. Why didn't they start home until late in the afternoon?

	Tick **one**
It was very busy in town.	
The master's business took a long time.	
The weather slowed them down.	
They couldn't find what they were looking for.	

3. **Circle** the correct option to complete each sentence below:

a) The fallen branch landed

on the cart	on the horse
on the road	in the river

b) When the tree branch fell, Black Beauty reacted by

jumping	trembling
running off	neighing

c) After the tree branch fell, the men

drove around it	drove over it
moved it out of the way	turned around to go another way

4. Why did the horse stop when crossing the bridge even though his master instructed him to go on?

_____

_____

Classic Children's Literature for KS2

Summary — Black Beauty

1. *"Master said, God had given men reason, by which they could find out things for themselves; but he had given animals knowledge which did not depend on reason, and which was much more prompt and perfect in its way, and by which they had often saved the lives of men."*

In your own words, explain what the master was saying about men and animals.

_____
_____
_____
_____

2. Below are some summaries of different paragraphs from this text. **Number them 1–6** to show the order in which they appear in the text. The first one has been done for you.

A tree branch broke off and blocked the road.	
They all arrived home safely.	
On a windy, autumn day, the horse took his master on a journey for business.	1
They drove back to the crossroads towards the wooden bridge.	
The storm got worse and the river was rising.	
Beauty refused to cross the bridge.	

3. Which is the main message of this extract?

	Tick **one**
Don't go out in a storm.	
Humans are smarter than animals.	
Humans should trust animals' instincts.	
Always check before you cross a bridge.	

Inference — Black Beauty

1. Look at the paragraph beginning, *"The words were scarcely..."*.
What impression does this paragraph give you of the horse's character?

_____
_____
_____
_____

2. Look at the paragraph beginning, *'"Thank God!" said my master.'*
Put a **tick** in the correct box to show whether each of the following statements is a **fact** or **opinion**.

	Fact	Opinion
If they had carried on across the bridge, they would have fallen in the river.		
The storm was frightening.		
Black Beauty was an animal of great value.		
The men were very grateful to Black Beauty.		

3. Look at the paragraph beginning, *'"Thank God!" said my master.'* What are **two** ways the men show that they were shocked by the near miss at the bridge.

1. _____
2. _____

4. Look at the paragraph beginning, *"At last we came..."*.
Write **one** word that best describes how the mistress had been feeling.

_____

5. How do the two men feel about the horse at the end of the extract? **Use evidence** from the text to support your answer.

_____

Classic Children's Literature Years 5–6

Prediction Black Beauty

1. Based on what you have read, what will happen the next time the master takes the horse out on a journey?
Use evidence from the text to support your prediction.

_____
_____
_____
_____
_____
_____

2. Do you think the master will go out in a storm in the future?

	Tick **one**
yes	
no	
maybe	

Make a reasonable prediction with reference to the text.

_____
_____
_____
_____
_____

Text Meaning — Black Beauty

1. Draw lines to match each part of the story with the correct quotation from the text.

- setting
- character description
- action
- speech

- "I wish we were well out of this wood..."
- ...he gave me a sharp cut.
- John went with his master.
- There had been a great deal of rain...

2. From whose point of view is the story told?
_____

Is this effective? Give reasons for your answer.
_____
_____
_____
_____
_____

Classic Children's Literature Years 5–6

Author's Use of Language — Black Beauty

1. "...*the bottom was good...*"
What does this description suggest about the bottom of the river?
_____
_____

2. "...*I heard the master say to John that he had never been out in such a storm...*"
What impression of the storm does this give you?
_____
_____

3. Look at the paragraph beginning, "*The words were scarcely...*".
Find and **copy four different words** that create the image of a wild storm.
1. _____
2. _____
3. _____
4. _____

4. "...*tossing the torch about like one mad.*"
What does this description suggest about the man at the tollgate?
_____
_____

5. Look at the final four paragraphs. **Find** and **copy three phrases** that tell you what time of day it is when they arrive home.
1. _____
2. _____
3. _____

© Brilliant Publications Limited

Classic Children's Literature Years 5–6

Compare and Contrast — Black Beauty

1. How does the weather differ at the beginning and the end of the extract?
   _____
   _____

2. "...*if your Black Beauty had not been wiser than we were...*"
   In what way was Black Beauty wiser than the men?
   _____
   _____

3. How are the master and his wife different?
   _____
   _____

4. How are the characters of the master and John similar?
   _____
   _____

The Secret Garden

by Frances Hodgson Burnett

The skipping-rope was a wonderful thing. She counted and skipped, and skipped and counted, until her cheeks were quite red, and she was more interested than she had ever been since she was born. The sun was shining and a little wind was blowing,—not a rough wind, but one which came in delightful little gusts and brought a fresh scent of newly turned earth with it. She skipped round the fountain garden, and up one walk and down another. She skipped at last into the kitchen-garden and saw Ben Weatherstaff digging and talking to his robin, which was hopping about him. She skipped down the walk toward him and he lifted his head and looked at her with a curious expression. She had wondered if he would notice her. She wanted him to see her skip.

"Well!" he exclaimed. "Upon my word. P'raps tha' art a young 'un, after all, an' p'raps tha's got child's blood in thy veins instead of sour buttermilk. Tha's skipped red into thy cheeks as sure as my name's Ben Weatherstaff. I wouldn't have believed tha' could do it."

"I never skipped before," Mary said. "I'm just beginning. I can only go up to twenty."

"Tha' keep on," said Ben. "Tha' shapes well enough at it for a young 'un that's lived with heathen. Just see how he's watchin' thee," jerking his head toward the robin. "He followed after thee yesterday. He'll be at it again today. He'll be bound to find out what th' skippin'-rope is. He's never seen one. Eh!" shaking his head at the bird, "tha' curiosity will be th' death of thee sometime if tha' doesn't look sharp." Mary skipped round all the gardens and round the orchard, resting every few minutes. At length she went to her own special walk and made up her mind to try if she could skip the whole length of it. It was a good long skip and she began slowly, but before she had gone half-way down the path she was so hot and breathless that she was obliged to stop. She did not mind much, because she had already counted up to thirty. She stopped with a little laugh of pleasure, and there, lo and behold, was the robin swaying on a long branch of ivy. He had followed her and he greeted her with a chirp. As Mary had skipped toward him she felt something heavy in her pocket strike against her at each jump, and when she saw the robin she laughed again.

© Brilliant Publications Limited

Classic Children's Literature Years 5–6

"You showed me where the key was yesterday," she said. "You ought to show me the door today; but I don't believe you know!"

The robin flew from his swinging spray of ivy on to the top of the wall and he opened his beak and sang a loud, lovely trill, merely to show off. Nothing in the world is quite as adorably lovely as a robin when he shows off,—and they are nearly always doing it.

Mary Lennox had heard a great deal about Magic in her Ayah's stories, and she always said that what happened almost at that moment was Magic.

One of the nice little gusts of wind rushed down the walk, and it was a stronger one than the rest. It was strong enough to wave the branches of the trees, and it was more than strong enough to sway the trailing sprays of untrimmed ivy hanging from the wall. Mary had stepped close to the robin, and suddenly the gust of wind swung aside some loose ivy trails, and more suddenly still she jumped toward it and caught it in her hand. This she did because she had seen something under it,—a round knob which had been covered by the leaves hanging over it. It was the knob of a door.

She put her hands under the leaves and began to pull and push them aside. Thick as the ivy hung, it nearly all was a loose and swinging curtain, though some had crept over wood and iron. Mary's heart began to thump and her hands to shake a little in her delight and excitement. The robin kept singing and twittering away and tilting his head on one side, as if he were as excited as she was. What was this under her hands which was square and made of iron and which her fingers found a hole in?

It was the lock of the door which had been closed ten years and she put her hand in her pocket, drew out the key and found it fitted the keyhole. She put the key in and turned it. It took two hands to do it, but it did turn. And then she took a long breath and looked behind her up the long walk to see if any one was coming. No one was coming. No one ever did come, it seemed, and she took another long breath, because she could not help it, and she held back the swinging curtain of ivy and pushed back the door which opened slowly,—slowly.

Then she slipped through it, and shut it behind her, and stood with her back against it, looking about her and breathing quite fast with excitement, and wonder, and delight.

She was standing inside the secret garden.

Vocabulary — The Secret Garden

1. *"Tha' shapes well enough at it for a young 'un that's lived with heathen..."*
What does "Tha' shapes well enough at it" mean in this sentence?

	Tick **one**
can skip fast enough	
can make shapes with her body	
has learned to skip fast enough	
is skilled enough at turning the skipping rope	

2. *"Tha' shapes well enough at it for a young 'un that's lived with heathen..."*
Which word is closest in meaning to heathen?

	Tick **one**
nonbelievers	
family	
foreigners	
friends	

3. *"...but before she had gone half-way down the path she was so hot and breathless that she was obliged to stop."*
What does obliged to stop mean?
_____
_____

4. Look at the paragraph beginning, *"Tha' keep on..."*.
Find and **copy one word** from the text that is the closest in meaning to nodding.
_____

5. **Find** and **copy a group of words** that tells you Mary is expecting the robin to show her the door that fits the key.
_____

Classic Children's Literature Years 5–6

Retrieval — The Secret Garden

1. What was Ben Weatherstaff doing as he spoke to Mary?

	Tick **one**
picking vegetables	
planting seeds	
digging in the kitchen-garden	
sweeping the path	

2. **Circle** the correct word or phrase to complete the sentences below.
   a) Mary had a _____ in her pocket.

rock	key
skipping rope	coin

   b) The robin was showing off by _____ .

singing loudly	showing Mary the door
flying back and forth	sitting on the wall

3. What is the 'magic' that happened to Mary in this extract?
   _____
   _____

4. Using information from the text, put a tick in the correct box to show whether each statement is **true** or **false**.

	True	False
This was the first time Mary had used a skipping rope.		
Ben Weatherstaff gave Mary the key.		
Mary doesn't believe in magic.		
The wall was covered with holly.		

© Kate Heap and Brilliant Publications Limited

Classic Children's Literature for KS2

Summary — The Secret Garden

1. Which of the following would be the best summary of the whole text?

	Tick **one**
Finding the Key	
Skipping in the Garden	
The Secret Garden Found	
Magic in the Garden	

2. Below are some summaries of different paragraphs from this text. **Number them 1–6** to show the order in which they appear in the text. The first one has been done for you.

The robin followed Mary down the garden.	
Mary was enjoying skipping in the garden.	1
The wind blew the ivy on the wall.	
Mary turned the key in the lock.	
Mary found the door to the secret garden.	
Mary spoke with Ben Weatherstaff about her skipping.	

3. Using information from the text, **tick one box** in each row to show whether each statement is **true** or **false**.

	True	False
Mary enjoyed skipping.		
Ben and Mary were friendly with each other.		
Mary has a lot of space in which to play.		
Mary hoped she would find a door for the key.		

Classic Children's Literature Years 5–6

Inference — The Secret Garden

1. *"The skipping-rope was a wonderful thing."*
Why does the author say this? Refer to the text in your answer.
_____
_____

2. In the first paragraph, **find** and **copy one phrase** that shows that Mary felt proud of being able to skip.
_____
_____

3. What impression do you get of the robin's character? Refer to the text in your answer.
_____
_____

4. When the robin flew to the top of the wall and sang a loud, lovely trill, what do you think it was trying to say to Mary?
_____
_____

5. Look at the paragraph beginning, *"She put her hands under the leaves..."*.
Find and **copy three phrases** that show us Mary felt excited.
   1. _____
   2. _____
   3. _____

6. How do you know Mary was a bit uncertain about opening the door?
_____

© Brilliant Publications Limited   Classic Children's Literature Years 5–6

Prediction — The Secret Garden

1. Do you think Mary will continue to play out in the gardens on future days?

	Tick **one**
yes	
no	
maybe	

Make a reasonable prediction with reference to the text.

_____
_____
_____
_____
_____
_____

2. How would you react if you found a key and an unusual door? **Give reasons** for your answer.

_____
_____
_____
_____
_____

3. Based on what you have read in this extract, what do you think the rest of this book will be about?

Give reasons for your predictions.

_____
_____
_____
_____

Text Meaning — The Secret Garden

1. Draw lines to match each part of the story with the correct quotation from the text.

- character
- speech
- action
- dialect

- P'raps tha' art a young 'un, after all...
- "You showed me where the key was yesterday," she said,
- ...and he opened his beak and sang a loud, lovely trill, merely to show off.
- ...and suddenly a gust of wind swung aside some loose ivy trails...

Author's Use of Language — The Secret Garden

1. Ben Weatherstaff says, *"Upon my word. P'raps tha' art a young 'un, after all, an' p'raps tha's got child's blood in thy veins instead of sour buttermilk. Tha's skipped red into thy cheeks as sure as my name's Ben Weatherstaff. I wouldn't have believed tha' could do it."*

   Based on this comment, how do you think Mary had behaved previously?

   _____
   _____
   _____
   _____

2. Look at the first four paragraphs of the extract: *"The skipping-rope..."* to *"...she laughed again."*

   Find and **copy four different words** from these paragraphs that suggest Mary was enjoying herself.

   1. _____
   2. _____
   3. _____
   4. _____

3. *"Thick as the ivy hung, it nearly all was a loose and swinging curtain..."*

   What does <u>a loose and swinging curtain</u> suggest about the ivy?

   _____
   _____
   _____
   _____

Classic Children's Literature Years 5–6

Author's Use of Language — The Secret Garden

4. Read the paragraph beginning, *"It was the lock..."*.
Give **two** impressions this gives you of the lock?

1. _____
2. _____

5. What type of atmosphere is created in the last four paragraphs of the extract? **Use evidence** from the text to support your answer.

_____
_____
_____
_____

Compare and Contrast — The Secret Garden

1. How does Mary's mood change from the beginning to the end of the extract?
   _____
   _____
   _____

2. How are the characters of Mary and the robin similar?
   _____
   _____
   _____

3. Mary's Ayah (nursery maid / governess) told her stories about magic. Name **one** story you think she may have told Mary and **explain why**.
   _____
   _____
   _____
   _____

4. What is the most thought-provoking moment of the story? **Explain why** you think this.
   _____
   _____
   _____

The Jungle Book

by Rudyard Kipling

The Law of the Jungle, which never orders anything without a reason, forbids every beast to eat Man except when he is killing to show his children how to kill, and then he must hunt outside the hunting-grounds of his pack or tribe. The real reason for this is that man-killing means, sooner or later, the arrival of white men on elephants, with guns, and hundreds of brown men with gongs and rockets and torches. Then everybody in the jungle suffers. The reason the beasts give among themselves is that Man is the weakest and most defenseless of all living things, and it is unsportsmanlike to touch him. They say too,—and it is true,—that man-eaters become mangy, and lose their teeth.

The purr grew louder, and ended in the full-throated "Aaarh!" of the tiger's charge.

Then there was a howl—an untigerish howl—from Shere Khan. "He has missed," said Mother Wolf. "What is it?"

Father Wolf ran out a few paces and heard Shere Khan muttering and mumbling savagely as he tumbled about in the scrub.

"The fool has had no more sense than to jump at a woodcutter's campfire, so he has burned his feet," said Father Wolf, with a grunt. "Tabaqui is with him."

"Something is coming uphill," said Mother Wolf, twitching one ear. "Get ready."

The bushes rustled a little in the thicket, and Father Wolf dropped with his haunches under him, ready for his leap. Then, if you had been watching, you would have seen the most wonderful thing in the world,—the wolf checked in mid-spring. He made his bound before he saw what it was he was jumping at, and then he tried to stop himself. The result was that he shot up straight into the air for four or five feet, landing almost where he left the ground.

"Man!" he snapped. "A man's cub. Look!"

Directly in front of him, holding on by a low branch, stood a naked brown baby who could just walk,—as soft and as dimpled a little thing as ever came to a wolf's cave at night. He looked up into Father Wolf's face and laughed.

"Is that a man's cub?" said Mother Wolf. "I have never seen one. Bring it here."

A wolf accustomed to moving his own cubs can, if necessary, mouth an egg without breaking it, and though Father Wolf's jaws closed right on the child's back not a tooth even scratched the skin, as he laid it down among the cubs.

"How little! How naked, and,—how bold!" said Mother Wolf, softly. The baby was pushing his way between the cubs to get close to the warm hide. "Ahai! He is taking his meal with the others. And so this is a man's cub. Now, was there ever a wolf that could boast of a man's cub among her children?"

"I have heard now and again of such a thing, but never in our pack or in my time," said Father Wolf. "He is altogether without hair, and I could kill him with a touch of my foot. But see, he looks up and is not afraid."

The moonlight was blocked out of the mouth of the cave, for Shere Khan's great square head and shoulders were thrust into the entrance. Tabaqui, behind him, was squeaking: "My Lord, my Lord, it went in here!"

"Shere Khan does us great honor," said Father Wolf, but his eyes were very angry. "What does Shere Khan need?"

"My quarry. A man's cub went this way," said Shere Khan. "Its parents have run off. Give it to me."

Shere Khan had jumped at a wood-cutter's camp-fire, as Father Wolf had said, and was furious from the pain of his burned feet. But Father Wolf knew that the mouth of the cave was too narrow for a tiger to come in by. Even where he was, Shere Khan's shoulders and fore paws were cramped for want of room, as a man's would be if he tried to fight in a barrel.

"The Wolves are a free people," said Father Wolf. "They take orders from the Head of the Pack, and not from any striped cattle-killer. The man's cub is ours – to kill if we choose."

"Ye choose and ye do not choose! What talk is this of choosing? By the Bull that I killed, am I to stand nosing into your dog's den for my fair dues? It is I, Shere Khan, who speak!"

The tiger's roar filled the cave with thunder. Mother Wolf shook herself clear of the cubs and sprang forward, her eyes, like two green moons in the darkness, facing the blazing eyes of Shere Khan.

"And it is I, Raksha [the Demon], who answers. The man's cub is mine, Lungri—mine to me! He shall not be killed. He shall live to run with the Pack and to hunt with the Pack; and in the end, look you, hunter of little naked cubs—frog-eater—fish-killer, he shall hunt thee! Now get hence, or by the Sambhur that I killed (I eat no starved cattle), back thou goest to thy mother, burned beast of the jungle, lamer than ever thou camest into the world! Go!"

Father Wolf looked on amazed. He had almost forgotten the days when he won Mother Wolf in fair fight from five other wolves, when she ran in the Pack and was not called the Demon for compliment's sake. Shere Khan might have faced Father Wolf, but he could not stand up against Mother Wolf, for he knew that where he was she had all the advantage

of the ground, and would fight to the death. So he backed out of the cave-mouth growling, and when he was clear he shouted:

"Each dog barks in his own yard! We will see what the Pack will say to this fostering of man-cubs. The cub is mine, and to my teeth he will come in the end, O bush-tailed thieves!"

Mother Wolf threw herself down panting among the cubs, and Father Wolf said to her gravely:

"Shere Khan speaks this much truth. The cub must be shown to the Pack. Wilt thou still keep him, Mother?"

"Keep him!" she gasped. "He came naked, by night, alone and very hungry; yet he was not afraid! Look, he has pushed one of my babes to one side already. And that lame butcher would have killed him, and would have run off to the Waingunga while the villagers here hunted through all our lairs in revenge! Keep him? Assuredly I will keep him. Lie still, little frog. O thou Mowgli,—for Mowgli, the Frog, I will call thee,—the time will come when thou wilt hunt Shere Khan as he has hunted thee!"

Vocabulary — The Jungle Book

1. Choose the best definition for <u>forbids</u>.

	Tick **one**
warns not to do something	
suggests not to	
refuses to allow	
permits	

2. In the first paragraph, **which word** could best replace <u>mangy</u>? **Circle one**.

hungry	unhappy	dirty	diseased

3. In the paragraph beginning, "*The bushes rustled...*", **find** and **copy one word** that means the wolf held back.

   _____

4. **Find** and **copy a synonym** for <u>prey</u>.

   _____

5. "*Mother wolf threw herself down panting among the cubs, and Father Wolf said to her gravely...*"

   What does the word <u>panting</u> tell the reader about how Mother Wolf was feeling after confronting Shere Khan?

   _____

   _____

6. **Which word** best sums up how Mother Wolf treated Mowgli? **Circle one**.

patience	rejection	acceptance	indifference

© Brilliant Publications Limited

Classic Children's Literature Years 5–6

Retrieval — The Jungle Book

1. What happens to man-eaters in the jungle?
   _____
   _____

2. Why did Father Wolf shoot *"straight up into the air for four or five feet, landing almost where he left the ground"*?
   _____
   _____

3. What does the man's cub do as soon as Father Wolf brings him over to Mother Wolf?
   _____
   _____

4. Why was Shere Khan not able to catch the man's cub in the first place?
   _____
   _____

5. What must the wolves do with the man's cub before they can decide to keep it?
   _____
   _____

6. Using information from the text, put a tick in the correct box to show whether each statement is **true** or **false**.

	True	False
The wolves heard Shere Khan capture his prey.		
Father Wolf attacked the animal rustling in the bushes.		
The man's cub was wearing clothes.		
Shere Khan came right into the wolves' cave.		

Summary   The Jungle Book

1. Look at the first paragraph. What is the **real reason** for the law forbidding beasts from eating men? **Explain** in your own words with reference to the text.

_____
_____
_____
_____

2. Which of the following would be the best title for this text?

	Tick **one**
The Law of the Jungle	
Shere Khan Attacks	
Unafraid	
The Newest Member of the Wolf Pack	

Explain your choice with reference to the text.

_____
_____
_____
_____
_____

Inference — The Jungle Book

1. Look at the first paragraph.
Why do the animals need the Law of the Jungle?

_____

2. "He looked up into Father Wolf's face and laughed."
What impression does this sentence give of the man's cub?

_____

3. "Shere Khan does us great honor..."
Does Father Wolf really mean what he says?

	Tick **one**
yes	
no	

Explain how you know with reference to the text.

_____
_____

4. Look at the paragraph beginning, "And it is I, Raksha..."
Why does Mother Wolf call Shere Khan "hunter of little naked cubs — frog-eater — fish-killer..."?

_____
_____

Inference   The Jungle Book

5. *"Father wolf looked on amazed."*
How does he feel about his partner?

	Tick **one**
shocked	
respectful	
embarrassed	
confused	

6. Mother Wolf was known as "Demon" by the wolf pack. What impressions does this name give you of her character? Give evidence to support your answers.

Impression	Evidence

Classic Children's Literature Years 5–6

Prediction — The Jungle Book

1. What does Mother Wolf predict Mowgli will do in the future?

2. If the man's cub had been killed by Shere Khan, what would have happened to the animals of the jungle? **Explain** fully with reference to the text.

Text Meaning — The Jungle Book

1. Draw lines to match each part of the story with the correct quotation from the text.

character	The moonlight was blocked out of the mouth of the cave...
speech	"Ye choose and ye do not choose!"
setting	Father Wolf ran out a few paces and heard Shere Khan muttering and mumbling savagely...
action	Then there was a howl — an untigerish howl —

2. Why do you think the author includes an explanation of the Law of the Jungle at the beginning of this text?

_____
_____
_____
_____
_____

© Brilliant Publications Limited

Author's Use of Language — The Jungle Book

1. *"Then there was a howl — an untigerish howl — from Shere Khan."*
   What does this phrase suggest about the tiger?
   _____
   _____
   _____

2. Mother Wolf describes the man's cub as, *"How little! How naked, and — how bold!"* Using the whole text, **find two examples** on the man's cub acting bold.

   1. _____
   2. _____

Classic Children's Literature Years 5–6

Author's Use of Language — The Jungle Book

3. *"They take orders from the Head of the Pack, and not from any striped cattle-killer."*
Why does Father Wolf use the phrase *"striped cattle-killer"*?
_____
_____
_____

4. In the paragraph beginning, *"And it is I, Raksha (the Demon)…"*, Mother Wolf is speaking to Shere Khan. Why does she use the phrase *"lamer than ever thou camest into the world"*? Make reference to the text in your answer.
_____
_____
_____

5. Shere Khan intends to kill the man's cub eventually. **Find** and **copy the phrase** that tells the reader this.
_____
_____
_____

6. Mother Wolf gives the man's cub the name Mowgli, the Frog. What does this tell the reader about his character?
_____
_____
_____

Compare and Contrast — The Jungle Book

1. *"The reason the beasts give among themselves is that Man is the weakest and most defenceless of all living things, and it is unsportsmanlike to touch him."*
Why do you think the animals tell each other the reason above instead of the real reason that if they kill men, more men will come to hunt the animals?

_____
_____
_____
_____

2. In the paragraph beginning, *"The tiger's roar filled the cave..."*, the author compares Mother Wolf with Shere Khan's eyes.
a) How are they different?

_____
_____
_____

b) How are they similar?

_____
_____
_____

3. In the paragraph beginning, *"And it is I, Raksha..."*, Mother Wolf refers to herself and Shere Khan by special names: Raksha and Lungri (meaning *"lame one"*). How are these names different in their meaning?

_____
_____
_____

4. How will the man's cub end up similar to Shere Khan as he grows up?

_____
_____
_____

Classic Children's Literature Years 5–6

Treasure Island

by Robert Louis Stevenson

SQUIRE TRELAWNEY, Dr. Livesey, and the rest of these gentlemen having asked me to write down the whole particulars about Treasure Island, from the beginning to the end, keeping nothing back but the bearings of the island, and that only because there is still treasure not yet lifted, I take up my pen in the year of grace 17— and go back to the time when my father kept the Admiral Benbow inn and the brown old seaman with the sabre cut first took up his lodging under our roof.

I remember him as if it were yesterday, as he came plodding to the inn door, his sea-chest following behind him in a hand-barrow – a tall, strong, heavy, nut-brown man, his tarry pigtail falling over the shoulder of his soiled blue coat, his hands ragged and scarred, with black, broken nails, and the sabre cut across one cheek, a dirty, livid white. I remember him looking round the cover and whistling to himself as he did so, and then breaking out in that old sea-song that he sang so often afterwards:

"Fifteen men on the dead man's chest—
Yo-ho-ho, and a bottle of rum!"

in the high, old tottering voice that seemed to have been tuned and broken at the capstan bars. Then he rapped on the door with a bit of stick like a handspike that he carried, and when my father appeared, called roughly for a glass of rum. This, when it was brought to him, he drank slowly, like a connoisseur, lingering on the taste and still looking about him at the cliffs and up at our signboard.

"This is a handy cove," says he at length; "and a pleasant sittyated grog-shop. Much company, mate?"

My father told him no, very little company, the more was the pity.

"Well, then," said he, "this is the berth for me. Here you, matey," he cried to the man who trundled the barrow; "bring up alongside and help up my chest. I'll stay here a bit," he continued. "I'm a plain man; rum and bacon and eggs is what I want, and that head up there for to watch ships off. What you mought call me? You mought call me captain. Oh, I see what you're at—there"; and he threw down three or four gold pieces on the threshold. "You can tell me when I've worked through that," says he, looking as fierce as a commander.

And indeed bad as his clothes were and coarsely as he spoke, he had none of the appearance of a man who sailed before the mast, but seemed like a mate or skipper accustomed to be obeyed or to strike. The man who came with the barrow told us the mail had set him down the morning before at the Royal George, that he had inquired what inns there were along the coast, and hearing ours well spoken of, I suppose, and described as lonely, had chosen it from the others for his place of residence. And that was all we could learn of our guest.

He was a very silent man by custom. All day he hung round the cove or upon the cliffs with a brass telescope; all evening he sat in a corner of the parlour next the fire and drank rum and water very strong. Mostly he would not speak when spoken to, only look up sudden and fierce and blow through his nose like a fog-horn; and we and the people who came about our house soon learned to let him be. Every day when he came back from his stroll he would ask if any seafaring men had gone by along the road. At first we thought it was the want of company of his own kind that made him ask this question, but at last we began to see he was desirous to avoid them. When a seaman did put up at the Admiral Benbow (as now and then some did, making by the coast road for Bristol) he would look in at him through the curtained door before he entered the parlour; and he was always sure to be as silent as a mouse when any such was present. For me, at least, there was no secret about the matter, for I was, in a way, a sharer in his alarms. He had taken me aside one day and promised me a silver fourpenny on the first of every month if I would only keep my "weather-eye open for a seafaring man with one leg" and let him know the moment he appeared. Often enough when the first of the month came round and I applied to him for my wage, he would only blow through his nose at me and stare me down, but before the week was out he was sure to think better of it, bring me my four-penny piece, and repeat his orders to look out for "the seafaring man with one leg."

How that personage haunted my dreams, I need scarcely tell you. On stormy nights, when the wind shook the four corners of the house and the surf roared along the cove and up the cliffs, I would see him in a thousand forms, and with a thousand diabolical expressions. Now the leg would be cut off at the knee, now at the hip; now he was a monstrous kind of a creature who had never had but the one leg, and that in the middle of his body. To see him leap and run and pursue me over hedge and ditch was the worst of nightmares. And altogether I paid pretty dear for my monthly fourpenny piece, in the shape of these abominable fancies.

Vocabulary — Treasure Island

1. "...*keeping nothing back but the bearings of the island...*"
Which word is closest in meaning to <u>bearings</u>?

	Tick **one**
map	
description	
location	
picture	

2. In the first paragraph, **find** and **copy one word** that tells you the old seaman was going to stay at the inn.

_____

3. In the third paragraph beginning, "*...in the high, old tottering voice...*", **find** and **copy the word** that is closest in meaning to <u>expert</u>.

_____

4. What does the old seaman mean by "*a pleasant sittyated grog-shop*"?

_____
_____
_____

5. In the paragraph beginning, "*And indeed bad as his clothes were...*" **which phrase** could replace the word <u>mail</u>?

	Tick **one**
postal delivery	
train	
horse-drawn coach	
postal lorry	

Classic Children's Literature Years 5–6 © Brilliant Publications Limited

Retrieval — Treasure Island

1. Why will the narrator not give the bearings of the island?
   _____

2. **Find** and **copy three words or phrases** to describe the old seaman.
   1. _____
   2. _____
   3. _____

3. Using information from the text, **tick one box** in each row to show whether each statement is **true** or **false**.

	True	False
The seaman was on his own when he arrived at the inn.		
The seaman had a scar on his face.		
The seaman chose the inn because it was popular.		
The narrator was paid a silver fourpenny each week to watch out for the man with one leg.		

4. **Circle** the correct option to answer each question below.

a) What was the name of the inn?

| Admiral Benbow | Squire Trelawney | Treasure Island | The Old Seaman |

b) The old seaman had been cut by a ...

| sword | dagger | sabre | knife |

c) The seaman wanted everyone to call him...

| commander | skipper | mate | captain |

d) All day the old seaman...

| drank rum | sang old sea-songs | watched for ships | sat by the fire |

Summary — Treasure Island

1. Below are some summaries of different paragraphs from this text. **Number them 1–6** to show the order in which they appear in the text. The last one (6) has been done for you.

The old seaman spent time at the cove and upon the cliffs with his telescope.	
The old seaman arrived at the inn.	
The old seaman gave the innkeeper gold pieces to pay for his room and food.	
The old seaman arrived in the town to look for a suitable inn.	
The narrator had nightmares about the man with one leg.	6
The old seaman asked about the popularity of the inn.	

2. Using information from the text, **tick one box** in each row to show whether each statement is **true** or **false**.

	True	False
The narrator was a bit afraid of the old seaman.		
The seaman was nervous around strangers.		
The seaman was like all the other guests at the inn.		
Thoughts of the old seaman caused nightmares for the narrator.		

Inference — Treasure Island

1. Why did the old seaman ask if there was much company at the inn?

	Tick **one**
He didn't want to be found.	
He was looking for someone.	
He wanted to meet new people.	
He was waiting for a friend.	

2. When the old seaman came back from his strolls, what **two** things did he do that showed he did not want to meet other sailors?

1. _____
2. _____

3. Look at the paragraph beginning, *"He was a very silent..."*. **Find** and **copy two words or phrases** that show the old seaman was very mysterious.

1. _____
2. _____

4. How did the narrator feel about having the old seaman at the inn? **Use evidence** from the text in your answer.

_____
_____
_____
_____

5. Why did the *"man with one leg"* take on so many forms in the narrator's nightmares?

_____
_____

© Brilliant Publications Limited

Classic Children's Literature Years 5–6

Prediction Treasure Island

1. Why do you think the old seaman was *"desirous to avoid"* other seafaring men?
Make reference to the text in your answer.

_____
_____
_____
_____
_____

2. Would you like to meet the old seaman?

	Tick **one**
yes	
no	
maybe	

Make reference to the text in your answer.

_____
_____
_____
_____

Text Meaning — Treasure Island

1. Draw lines to match each part of the story with the correct quotation from the text.

speech	On stormy nights, when the wind shook the four corners of the house...
setting	...he drank slowly, like a connoisseur, lingering on the taste...
action	...keep my 'weather-eye open for a seafaring man with one leg'
character	...his hands ragged and scarred, with black, broken nails

Author's Use of Language — Treasure Island

1. *"Fifteen men on the dead man's chest —*
   Yo-ho-ho, and a bottle of rum!"

   What impression does this give you of the old seaman?

   _____
   _____
   _____
   _____

2. Two different similes are used to describe the old seaman. **Find** and **copy one simile** then explain what it suggests about the man.

   Simile: _____

   _____
   _____

3. **Find** and **copy a phrase** that suggests that he was not just an ordinary sailor.

   _____
   _____

4. Look at the final paragraph of the extract.
   Find and **copy four different words** from this paragraph that suggest the man with one leg is frightening.

   1. _____ 2. _____
   3. _____ 4. _____

5. *"... paid pretty dear for my monthly fourpenny piece."*
   What does this suggest about the narrator?

   _____
   _____

Classic Children's Literature Years 5–6   © Brilliant Publications Limited

Compare and Contrast — Treasure Island

1. Do you think the old seaman is a pirate?

	Tick **one**
yes	
no	
maybe	

Use evidence from the text to support your answer.

_____
_____
_____
_____

2. Look at the paragraph beginning, "*He was a very silent man…*".
How does the narrator's impression of the old seaman change during this paragraph?

_____
_____
_____
_____

Classic Children's Literature Years 5–6

Twenty Thousand Leagues Under The Sea

by Jules Verne

THE NEXT DAY, March 22, at six o'clock in the morning, preparations for departure began. The last gleams of twilight were melting into night. The cold was brisk. The constellations were glittering with startling intensity. The wonderful Southern Cross, polar star of the Antarctic regions, twinkled at its zenith.

The thermometer marked -12 degrees centigrade, and a fresh breeze left a sharp nip in the air. Ice floes were increasing over the open water. The sea was starting to congeal everywhere. Numerous blackish patches were spreading over its surface, announcing the imminent formation of fresh ice. Obviously this southernmost basin froze over during its six-month winter and became utterly inaccessible. What happened to the whales during this period? No doubt they went beneath the Ice Bank to find more feasible seas. As for seals and walruses, they were accustomed to living in the harshest climates and stayed on in these icy waterways. These animals know by instinct how to gouge holes in the ice fields and keep them continually open; they go to these holes to breathe. Once the birds have migrated northward to escape the cold, these marine mammals remain as sole lords of the polar continent.

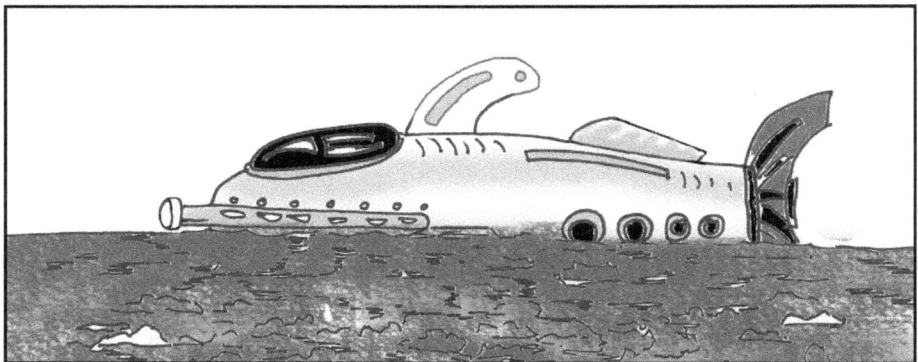

Meanwhile the ballast tanks filled with water and the Nautilus sank slowly. At a depth of 1,000 feet, it stopped. Its propeller churned the waves and it headed due north at a speed of fifteen miles per hour. Near the afternoon it was already cruising under the immense frozen carapace of the Ice Bank.

As a precaution, the panels in the lounge stayed closed, because the Nautilus's hull could run afoul of some submerged block of ice. So I spent the day putting my notes into final form. My mind was completely wrapped up in my memories of the pole. We had reached that inaccessible spot without facing exhaustion or danger, as if our seagoing passenger carriage had glided there on railroad tracks. And now we had actually started our return journey. Did it still have comparable surprises in store for me? I felt sure it did, so inexhaustible is this series of underwater wonders! As it was, in the five and a half months since fate had brought us on board, we had cleared 14,000 leagues, and over this track longer than the earth's equator, so many fascinating or frightening incidents had beguiled our voyage: that hunting trip in the Crespo forests, our running aground in the Torres Strait, the coral cemetery, the pearl fisheries of Ceylon, the Arabic tunnel, the fires of Santorini, those millions in the Bay of Vigo, Atlantis, the South Pole! During the night all these memories crossed over from one dream to the next, not giving my brain a moment's rest.

At three o'clock in the morning, I was awakened by a violent collision. I sat up in bed, listening in the darkness, and then was suddenly hurled into the middle of my stateroom. Apparently the Nautilus had gone aground, then heeled over sharply.

Leaning against the walls, I dragged myself down the gangways to the lounge, whose ceiling lights were on. The furniture had been knocked over. Fortunately the glass cases were solidly secured at the base and had stood fast. Since we were no longer vertical, the starboard pictures were glued to the tapestries, while those to port had their lower edges hanging a foot away from the wall. So the Nautilus was lying on its starboard side, completely stationary to boot.

In its interior I heard the sound of footsteps and muffled voices. But Captain Nemo didn't appear. Just as I was about to leave the lounge, Ned Land and Conseil entered.

"What happened?" I instantly said to them.

"I came to ask master that," Conseil replied.

"Damnation!" the Canadian exclaimed. "I know full well what happened! The Nautilus has gone aground, and judging from the way it's listing, I don't think it'll pull through like that first time in the Torres Strait."

"But," I asked, "are we at least back on the surface of the sea?"

"We have no idea," Conseil replied.

"It's easy to find out," I answered.

I consulted the pressure gauge. Much to my surprise, it indicated a depth of 360 meters.

"What's the meaning of this?" I exclaimed.

"We must confer with Captain Nemo," Conseil said.

"But where do we find him?" Ned Land asked.

"Follow me," I told my two companions.

We left the lounge. Nobody in the library. Nobody by the central companionway or the crew's quarters. I assumed that Captain Nemo was stationed in the pilothouse. Best to wait. The three of us returned to the lounge.

I'll skip over the Canadian's complaints. He had good grounds for an outburst. I didn't answer him back, letting him blow off all the steam he wanted.

We had been left to ourselves for twenty minutes, trying to detect the tiniest noises inside the Nautilus, when Captain Nemo entered. He didn't seem to see us. His facial features, usually so emotionless, revealed a certain uneasiness. He studied the compass and pressure gauge in silence, then went and put his finger on the world map at a spot in the sector depicting the southernmost seas.

I hesitated to interrupt him. But some moments later, when he turned to me, I threw back at him a phrase he had used in the Torres Strait:

"An incident, captain?"

"No, sir," he replied, "this time an accident."

"Serious?"

"Perhaps."

"Is there any immediate danger?"

"No."

"The Nautilus has run aground?"

"Yes."

"And this accident came about… ?"

"Through nature's unpredictability not man's incapacity. No errors were committed in our manoeuvres. Nevertheless, we can't prevent a loss of balance from taking its toll. One may defy human laws, but no one can withstand the laws of nature."

Captain Nemo had picked an odd time to philosophise. All in all, this reply told me nothing.

"May I learn, sir," I asked him, "what caused this accident?"

"An enormous block of ice, an entire mountain, has toppled over," he answered me. "When an iceberg is eroded at the base by warmer waters or by repeated collisions, its center of gravity rises. Then it somersaults, it turns completely upside down. That's what happened here. When it overturned, one of these blocks hit the Nautilus as it was cruising under the waters. Sliding under our hull, this block then raised us with irresistible power, lifting us into less congested strata where we now lie on our side."

"But can't we float the Nautilus clear by emptying its ballast tanks, to regain our balance?"

"That, sir, is being done right now. You can hear the pumps working. Look at the needle on the pressure gauge. It indicates that the Nautilus is rising, but this block of ice is rising with us, and until some obstacle halts its upward movement, our position won't change."

Indeed, the Nautilus kept the same heel to starboard. No doubt it would straighten up once the block came to a halt. But before that happened, who knew if we might not hit the underbelly of the Ice Bank and be hideously squeezed between two frozen surfaces?

Vocabulary — Twenty Thousand Leagues Under the Sea

1. *"The last gleams of twilight were melting into night."*

What does the phrase <u>last gleams of twilight</u> suggest about the sky?

_____

_____

2. Look at the second paragraph beginning, *"The thermometer marked -12 degrees centigrade..."*.

Find and **copy one word or phrase** meaning:

a) absolutely unapproachable

_____

b) useable

_____

c) natural intuition

_____

d) hollow out

_____

e) always

_____

3. *"Meanwhile the ballast tanks filled with water and the Nautilus sank slowly."*

What does the word <u>ballast</u> mean in the sentence above?

	Tick **one**
float	
counterweight	
cargo	
ice	

Vocabulary — Twenty Thousand Leagues Under the Sea

4. *"The Nautilus has gone aground, and judging from the way it's listing, I don't think it'll pull through like that first time in the Torres Strait."*

What does the word <u>listing</u> mean in the sentence above?

	Tick **one**
falling	
stuck	
leaning	
stopping	

Retrieval — Twenty Thousand Leagues Under the Sea

1. Look at the first and second paragraphs. The Nautilus is in the Antarctic. **Find** and **copy two** facts that demonstrate that this is true.

    1. _____

    2. _____

2. Match the Antarctic animals to their survival methods:

    walruses — migrate northward to escape the cold

    birds — accustomed to staying on the icy waterways

    seals — go beneath the Ice Bank to find more feasible seas

    whales — gouge holes in the ice fields so they can breathe

3. Which animals are rulers of the Antarctic throughout the winter months?

_____

Retrieval — Twenty Thousand Leagues Under the Sea

4. a) How long had the author been on the Nautilus?
_____

b) How far had the author travelled on the Nautilus?
_____

5. What caused the author to wake in the middle of the night?

	Tick **one**
falling out of bed	
the clock striking three o'clock	
a violent collision	
the Nautilus heeled over sharply	

6. Using information from the text, put a **tick** in the correct box to show whether each statement is **true** or **false**.

	True	False
The glass cases had fallen over in the collision.		
This is the first time the Nautilus had gone aground.		
The Nautilus was still moving slowly.		
The Nautilus was leaning to its starboard side.		

7. Why isn't the Nautilus regaining balance as it empties its ballast tanks?
_____
_____

8. What is the author's fear as the Nautilus rises to the surface?
_____
_____

© Kate Heap and Brilliant Publications Limited

Classic Children's Literature for KS2

Summary — Twenty Thousand Leagues Under the Sea

1. Below are some summaries of different paragraphs from this text. **Number them 1–6** to show the order in which they appear in the text. The first one (1) has been done for you.

The author reflected on his time at sea.	
They tried to find out what had caused the collision.	
The Nautilus sank beneath the ice.	
They were worried they would become trapped between the Ice Bank and the piece of ice beneath them.	
The people on board the Nautilus were woken suddenly.	
The crew of the Nautilus prepared to depart the Antarctic region.	1

2. Look at the paragraph beginning, "*An enormous block of ice ...*".
In your own words, summarise what caused the accident.

_____
_____
_____
_____

3. Which of the following would be the best title for this text?

	Tick **one**
A Dangerous Incident	
A Frozen Night	
An Antarctic Accident	
Life on the Ice	

Classic Children's Literature Years 5–6

Inference — Twenty Thousand Leagues Under the Sea

1. Look at the first two paragraphs. Why is the crew of the Nautilus preparing to depart the Antarctic now?

_____
_____

2. What is the Nautilus? **Give evidence** from the text to support your answer.

_____
_____
_____

3. Look at the paragraph beginning, "*As a precaution, the panels in the lounge...*". How is the author feeling about his time on the Nautilus? **Give evidence** from the text to support your answer.

_____
_____
_____
_____
_____

4. "*I consulted the pressure gauge. Much to my surprise, it indicated a depth of 360 metres.*"

Why is the author surprised at this?

_____
_____
_____

5. Read on from the paragraph beginning, "*We had been left to ourselves...*". **Find one piece of evidence** to support each of the impressions below.

Impression	Evidence
Captain Nemo was anxious about the situation.	
Captain Nemo was a man of few words.	
Captain Nemo was very intelligent.	

Prediction

Twenty Thousand Leagues Under the Sea

1. Do you think the Nautilus will regain balance and travel to safety?

	Tick **one**
yes	
no	

   Use what you already know of the story to back up your prediction.

   _____
   _____

2. Will the author want to continue to travel on the Nautilus?

	Tick **one**
yes	
no	

   Explain your prediction with reference to the text.

   _____
   _____
   _____
   _____

Text Meaning

Twenty Thousand Leagues Under the Sea

1. Why does the author begin with a long section of narrative?
   _____
   _____

2. Where would you expect to find this extract in the full book of Twenty Thousand Leagues Under the Sea?

	Tick **one**
Near the beginning	
In the middle	
Near the end	

Why?
_____
_____
_____
_____

© Brilliant Publications Limited

Classic Children's Literature Years 5–6

Author's Use of Language

Twenty Thousand Leagues Under the Sea

1. In the first paragraph, the author paints a picture of the sky. The South Pole is just going into a season when the nights are becoming longer and longer – the sun hardly creeps above the horizon and it is *"twilight"* all day. How does the author show this through his description?

   _____
   _____
   _____

2. In the second paragraph, the author paints a picture of a frozen world. **Find four words** or **phrases** that contribute to this description.

   1. _____
   2. _____
   3. _____
   4. _____

3. What is the occupation of the narrator of the story? **Use evidence** from the text to support your answer.

   _____
   _____

4. Look at the paragraph beginning, "*As a precaution, the panels in the lounge...*".
   Find and **copy the simile** used to describe their journey to the Antarctic.

   _____
   _____

5. "*...this block then raised us with irresistible power...*"
   What does the phrase <u>irresistible power</u> tell you about the Antarctic ice?

   _____
   _____

Classic Children's Literature Years 5–6

Compare and Contrast — Twenty Thousand Leagues Under the Sea

1. *"Near the afternoon it was already cruising under the immense frozen carapace of the Ice Bank."*
A carapace is the hard upper shell of a tortoise or crustacean.
Why does the author describe the ice as a <u>carapace</u>?

_____
_____
_____

2. How are Captain Nemo's and the Canadian's reaction to the collision different?

_____
_____
_____

3. Explain how methods for navigating the seas and identifying dangerous icebergs at the time of this story compare to methods used today.

_____
_____
_____

A Christmas Carol

by Charles Dickens

Marley was dead, to begin with. There is no doubt whatever about that. The register of his burial was signed by the clergyman, the clerk, the undertaker, and the chief mourner. Scrooge signed it. And Scrooge's name was good upon 'Change for anything he chose to put his hand to. Old Marley was as dead as a door-nail.'

Mind! I don't mean to say that I know, of my own knowledge, what there is particularly dead about a door-nail. I might have been inclined, myself, to regard a coffin-nail as the deadest piece of ironmongery in the trade. But the wisdom of our ancestors is in the simile; and my unhallowed hands shall not disturb it, or the Country's done for. You will, therefore, permit me to repeat, emphatically, that Marley was as dead as a door-nail.

Scrooge knew he was dead? Of course he did. How could it be otherwise? Scrooge and he were partners for I don't know how many years. Scrooge was his sole executor, his sole administrator, his sole assign, his sole residuary legatee, his sole friend, and sole mourner. And even Scrooge was not so dreadfully cut up by the sad event, but that he was an excellent man of business on the very day of the funeral, and solemnised it with an undoubted bargain.

The mention of Marley's funeral brings me back to the point I started from. There is no doubt that Marley was dead. This must be distinctly understood, or nothing wonderful can come of the story I am going to relate. If we were not perfectly convinced that Hamlet's Father died before the play began, there would be nothing more remarkable in his taking a stroll at night, in an easterly wind, upon his own ramparts, than there would be in any other middle-aged gentleman rashly turning out after dark in a breezy spot—say St. Paul's Church-yard, for instance—literally to astonish his son's weak mind.

Scrooge never painted out Old Marley's name. There it stood, years afterwards, above the warehouse door: Scrooge and Marley. The firm was known as Scrooge and Marley. Sometimes people new to the business called Scrooge Scrooge, and sometimes Marley, but he answered to both names. It was all the same to him.

Oh! but he was a tight-fisted hand at the grindstone, Scrooge! a squeezing, wrenching, grasping, scraping, clutching, covetous, old sinner! Hard and sharp as flint, from which no steel had ever struck out generous fire; secret, and self-contained, and solitary as an oyster. The cold within him froze his old features, nipped his pointed nose, shrivelled his cheek, stiffened his gait; made his eyes red, his thin lips blue; and spoke out shrewdly in his grating voice. A frosty rime was on his head, and on his eyebrows, and his wiry chin. He carried his own low temperature always about with him; he iced his office in the dog-days; and didn't thaw it one degree at Christmas.

External heat and cold had little influence on Scrooge. No warmth could warm, no wintry weather chill him. No wind that blew was bitterer than he, no falling snow was more intent upon its purpose, no pelting rain less open to entreaty. Foul weather didn't know where to have him. The heaviest rain, and snow, and hail, and sleet could boast of the advantage over him in only one respect. They often "came down" handsomely and Scrooge never did.

Nobody ever stopped him in the street to say, with gladsome looks, "My dear Scrooge, how are you? When will you come to see me?" No beggars implored him to bestow a trifle, no children asked him what it was o'clock, no man or woman ever once in all his life inquired the way to such and such a place, of Scrooge. Even the blind men's dogs appeared to know him; and, when they saw him coming on, would tug their owners into doorways and up courts; and then would wag their tails as though they said, "No eye at all is better than an evil eye, dark master!"

But what did Scrooge care? It was the very thing he liked. To edge his way along the crowded paths of life, warning all human sympathy to keep its distance, was what the knowing ones call "nuts" to Scrooge.

Once upon a time—of all the good days in the year, on Christmas Eve—old Scrooge sat busy in his counting-house. It was cold, bleak, biting weather: foggy withal: and he could hear the people in the court outside go wheezing up and down, beating their hands upon their breasts, and stamping their feet upon the pavement stones to warm them. The City clocks had only just gone three, but it was quite dark already—it had not been light all day—and candles were flaring in the windows of the neighbouring offices, like ruddy smears upon the palpable brown air. The fog came pouring in at every chink and keyhole, and was so dense without, that, although the court was of the narrowest, the houses opposite were mere phantoms. To see the dingy cloud come drooping down, obscuring everything, one might have thought that nature lived hard by and was brewing on a large scale.

The door of Scrooge's counting-house was open, that he might keep his eye upon his clerk, who in a dismal little cell beyond, a sort of tank, was copying letters. Scrooge had a very small fire, but the clerk's fire was so very much smaller that it looked like one coal. But he couldn't replenish it, for Scrooge kept the coal-box in his own room; and so surely as the clerk came in with the shovel, the master predicted that it would be necessary for them to part. Wherefore the clerk put on his white comforter, and tried to warm himself at the candle; in which effort, not being a man of strong imagination, he failed.

"A merry Christmas, uncle! God save you!" cried a cheerful voice. It was the voice of Scrooge's nephew, who came upon him so quickly that this was the first intimation he had of his approach.

"Bah!" said Scrooge. "Humbug!"

He had so heated himself with rapid walking in the fog and frost, this nephew of Scrooge's, that he was all in a glow; his face was ruddy and handsome; his eyes sparkled, and his breath smoked again.

"Christmas a humbug, uncle!" said Scrooge's nephew. "You don't mean that, I am sure?"

"I do," said Scrooge. "Merry Christmas! What right have you to be merry? What reason have you to be merry? You're poor enough."

"Come, then," returned the nephew gaily. "What right have you to be dismal? What reason have you to be morose? You're rich enough."

Scrooge, having no better answer ready on the spur of the moment, said, "Bah!" again; and followed it up with "Humbug!"

"Don't be cross, uncle!" said the nephew.

"What else can I be," returned the uncle, "when I live in such a world of fools as this? Merry Christmas! Out upon merry Christmas! What's Christmas-time to you but a time for paying bills without money; a time for finding yourself a year older, and not an hour richer; a time for balancing your books, and having every item in 'em through a round dozen of months presented dead against you? If I could work my will," said Scrooge indignantly, "every idiot who goes about with 'Merry Christmas' on his lips should be boiled with his own pudding, and buried with a stake of holly through his heart. He should!"

Vocabulary — A Christmas Carol

1. In the second paragraph, which word could best replace <u>emphatically</u>?
Circle one.

| enthusiastically | helpfully | hesitantly | without doubt |

2. In the paragraph beginning, "*Scrooge knew he was dead?*", what is the impact of the repetition of the word <u>sole</u>?

_____

3. In the paragraph beginning, "*Oh! but he was...*", **find** and **copy a synonym** for <u>frugal</u>.

_____

4. "*Oh! but he was a tight-fisted hand at the grindstone...*"
Choose the best definition for <u>grindstone</u> in this context.

	Tick **one**
hard, solid substance found in the ground that is often used for building	
focus on working hard at one's job	
someone or something that is extremely strong or reliable	
a large round stone used for sharpening knives and tools.	

5. "*A frosty rime was on his head, and on his eyebrows, and his wiry chin.*"
What does this tell us about Scrooge's hair?

_____

6. What does "*No eye at all is better than an evil eye*" mean?

	Tick **one**
The dogs can see Scrooge coming.	
The dogs don't want to look at Scrooge.	
The dogs run away from Scrooge.	
Being blind is better than being Scrooge.	

Classic Children's Literature Years 5–6   © Brilliant Publications Limited

Retrieval — A Christmas Carol

1. Why is there no doubt Marley was dead?
   _____

2. According to the narrator, who decides what similes should say?
   _____

3. In the paragraph beginning, "The mention of Marley's funeral...", why is it important that the reader knows Marley is dead?
   _____

4. Tick the illustration which best matches the description of the counting house sign.

Retrieval — A Christmas Carol

5. Using information from the text, put **a tick** in the correct box to show whether each statement is **true** or **false**.

	True	False
Children would ask Scrooge for the time.		
Scrooge walked along the sides of the crowds.		
This story takes place in Autumn.		
The city was covered in a thick fog.		

6. Why couldn't the clerk replenish his fire?

_____

_____

7. What is one of the reasons Scrooge gives for not liking Christmas?

	Tick **one**
He has to give his clerk the day off.	
It is a time for paying bills without money.	
He has to spend time with his family.	
He doesn't like holly.	

Summary — A Christmas Carol

1. Using information from the text, **write a summary** of the extract in 20 words or less.
   _____
   _____
   _____
   _____

2. Which of the following would be the best title for this text?

	Tick **one**
A Cold Christmas Eve	
Scrooge Alone	
Frosty and Friendless	
Miserable Miser	

   Explain your choice with reference to the text.
   _____
   _____
   _____

Classic Children's Literature Years 5–6

Inference — A Christmas Carol

1. Look at the third paragraph.
How did Scrooge feel about Marley's death? Use evidence from the text to support your answer.

2. Why was Scrooge proud of himself on the day of Marley's funeral? **Use evidence** from the text to support your answer.

3. In what form did Hamlet's father appear?

4. Look at the paragraph beginning, "*External heat and cold...*". **Find** and **copy three words or phrases** that could be used to describe Scrooge's personality.

5. Look at the paragraph beginning, "*Nobody ever stopped him in the street...*". What impression do you get of Scrooge's relationships with other people? Use evidence from the text to support your answer.

Classic Children's Literature Years 5–6

Prediction — A Christmas Carol

1. According to what you've read, will Scrooge always be alone?

	Tick **one**
yes	
no	

   Explain your prediction with reference to the text.
   _____
   _____
   _____

2. Does the emphasis on Marley being dead give any clues as to what might happen later in the story? Explain your answer with reference to the text.
   _____
   _____
   _____

© Brilliant Publications Limited

Classic Children's Literature Years 5–6

Text Meaning — A Christmas Carol

1. Draw lines to match each part of the story with the correct quotation from the text.

- metaphor
- simile
- setting
- character

- he was all in a glow; his face was ruddy and handsome
- from which no steel had ever struck out a generous fire
- dead as a door-nail
- of all the good days in the year, on Christmas Eve

2. Who is telling the story?
_____

3. How does the narrator feel about Scrooge?
_____

Author's Use of Language — A Christmas Carol

1. **Find** and **copy a simile** used to describe Marley.
   _____

2. Why might the author "*regard a coffin-nail as the deadest piece of ironmongery in the trade*"?
   _____
   _____

3. In the paragraph beginning, "*Oh! but he was...*", **find** and **copy four words** that suggest Scrooge has a horrible character.
   1. _____
   2. _____
   3. _____
   4. _____

4. In the paragraph beginning, "*Once upon a time...*", how does the setting description link to the mood of the story. **Make reference** to the text in your answer.
   _____
   _____

5. "*...every idiot who goes about with 'Merry Christmas' on his lips should be boiled in his own pudding and buried with a stake of holly through his heart.*"
   What is unexpected about this sentence?
   _____
   _____

© Brilliant Publications Limited

Classic Children's Literature Years 5–6

Compare and Contrast — A Christmas Carol

1. Does the character of Scrooge remind you of any other book or film character you have come across? Explain your answer with reference to the text.

   _____
   _____
   _____

2. In the paragraph beginning, *"Oh! but he was a tight-fisted..."*, to what is generosity compared?

   _____

3. In the same paragraph, to what object is Scrooge's mean character compared?

   _____

4. In this extract, we meet Scrooge and his nephew. How are they different?

   _____
   _____
   _____

5. In the paragraph beginning, *"'I do,' said Scrooge"*, he makes a comparison between a person's happiness and their wealth. What is the comparison?

   _____
   _____
   _____
   _____

Classic Children's Literature Years 5–6

Answers

Little House in the Big Woods (pages 13–24)

Little House in the Big Woods – Vocabulary
1. quivered
2. exchange
3. snatched / ran / slammed
4. She was sitting up late
5. fabric / cloth / material

Little House in the Big Woods – Retrieval
1. …snow was beginning to thaw.

    Bits of it dropped from the branches of the trees…

    …softening snowbanks…

    …drops of water hung trembling at their tips. (Referring to the icicles on the roof.)
2. one day
3. sunset
4. "Sukey is safe in the barn." because all those big, heavy logs in the barn walls. And the door is heavy and solid, made to keep bears out.
5.

	True	False
Pa went to town on horseback.		x
Pa brought presents for Laura, Mary and Ma.	x	
The bear tried to get into the house.		x
Sukey had escaped from the barn.		x

Little House in the Big Woods – Summary
1. A Frightening Surprise
2.

Pa prepared to go to town.	2
Laura went to help Ma with the milking.	5
The girls watched for Pa to come home.	3
Ma slapped the bear.	6
Ma started supper and did the chores.	4
Spring was coming.	1

Little House in the Big Woods – Inference
1. In the countryside / in the woods – "Laura and Mary had never seen a town."
2. It was usually a job for bigger children or adults. With Pa away, she was able to be more responsible and help Ma even more.
3. Sukey should have been shut up in the barn.
4. She was frightened by being so close to a bear that could have hurt them.

    She was relieved they had made it back to the house safely.

    She was worried that Sukey might be eaten by the bear.
5. Ma is worried that the bear might try to get into the house so she is pulling in the latch string to be safer.

6. It had been trying to get into the barn. There were bear tracks all around the barn and claw marks on the walls.

Little House in the Big Woods – Prediction
1. The bear was very large – it was the size of a cow. "She reached across the gate and slapped Sukey's shoulder."

   The bear might have become angry or frightened and attacked them. It could have chased them and hurt them. "But he could have hurt us…"

   It had very sharp claws. "…and there were marks of his claws on the walls."
2. Children's own answers supported by evidence from the text.

Little House in the Big Woods – Text Meaning
1. <u>speech</u>: "You were a good girl, Laura, to do exactly as I told you…"

   <u>character description</u>: Ma was trembling…

   <u>action</u>: …Pa strapped the bundle of furs on his shoulders…

   <u>setting</u>: Bits of it dropped from the branches of the trees…

Little House in the Big Woods – Author's Use of Language
1. She can't believe what has happened.
2. The wind crying sounds like it is sad and frightened. Laura feels the same way after her encounter with the bear.
3. She did a thing she had never done before.
4. The house had a lonely feeling because Pa wasn't there. It also seemed to be frightened because Pa wasn't there to protect them.

Little House in the Big Woods – Compare and Contrast
1. The stars did not look as warm and bright as the little lights that came from the lantern.
2. a) Sukey was about the same size as the bear.
   b) The bear was black while Sukey was brown.

   The bear had long, shaggy hair while Sukey had short hair.

   The bear had little, glittering eyes but Sukey had large, gentle eyes.
3. In the night Laura was frightened but in the morning, she was happy that Pa was there and, because he got good prices on his furs, he could bring them presents.

The Lion, the Witch and the Wardrobe (pages 25–36)

The Lion, the Witch and the Wardrobe – Vocabulary
1. heavy, nothing
2. radio
3. marched
4. inquisitive
5. in the midst of the trees

The Lion, the Witch and the Wardrobe – Retrieval
1. suit of armour / harp / balcony / very old books (bigger than a Bible in a church) / a big wardrobe / a dead blue-bottle
2.

3. 1) He carried several brown-paper parcels.
   2) Snow
4. 4
5.

	True	False
Lucy expected the wardrobe to be unlocked.		x
There were three rows of coats in the wardrobe.		x
Lucy could feel mothballs crunching underfoot.		x
The sun shone brightly in the woods.		x

The Lion, the Witch and the Wardrobe – Summary

1. The Way into Narnia
2.

Lucy walked to the lamp-post.	5
The children decided to explore the house.	2
Lucy spotted a Faun.	6
The children found many unexpected places.	3
The children had to play inside because of the rain.	1
Lucy decided to try the door of the wardrobe.	4

3.

	True	False
Lucy is more curious than her siblings.	x	
The rainy day led them to new adventures.	x	
The wardrobe was another "unexpected place".	x	
It was a rainy day in the woods inside the wardrobe.		x

The Lion, the Witch and the Wardrobe – Inference

1. curious: "…she thought it would be worth trying the door of the wardrobe…"
   independent: "…they all trooped out again, all except Lucy"
2. …arms stretched out in front of her…
   …bump her face on the back of the wardrobe.
   …expecting to feel woodwork against the tips of her fingers.
3. She keeps pushing away the coats expecting to find the back of the wardrobe.
4. To make sure she can find her way home.
5. Any option is acceptable if answer is supported by evidence from the text.

The Lion, the Witch and the Wardrobe – Prediction

1. Any option is acceptable if prediction is supported by evidence from the text.

The Lion, the Witch and the Wardrobe – Text Meaning

1. character: From the waist upwards he was like a man, but his legs were shaped like a goat's…

   rule: …she knew that it is very foolish to shut oneself into any wardrobe.

   onomatopoeia: …crunch-crunch over the snow and…

   action: …gave such a start of surprise that he dropped all his parcels.

The Lion, the Witch and the Wardrobe – Author's Use of Language

1. " There's a wireless, lots of books."
2. Magical, mysterious
3. They are very large. The Bible at the front of a church is often very big on a special stand.

4. It is soft and crumbly / dusty / fine / dry.
5. Small or tiny feet / light on its feet / stepping lightly / gentle / graceful

The Lion, the Witch and the Wardrobe – Compare and Contrast
1. Edmund is grumpy / negative / unhappy whereas/but/however Susan is positive / looks on the bright side / content.
2. At first, Lucy could feel the soft fur coats on her face but then it changed to hard, rough, prickly branches.
3. Lucy and the Faun are a similar height. They are both pleasant. They are both surprised.

Swallows and Amazons (pages 37–50)

Swallows and Amazons – Vocabulary
1. trembling
2. lapping
3. do reconnaissance
4. search carefully
5. Charge!
6. cautioned / warned
   whispered / commanded / instructed
   shouted / instructed / commanded

Swallows and Amazons – Retrieval
1. The sharp crack of a dead stick breaking somewhere in the middle of the island.
   Swallow was gone.
   There was a round place where the grass and ferns were pressed flat as if someone had been lying there.
   Roger found a knife.

2.

	True	False
A blow on the whistle means danger.		x
Three owl hoots mean they've found something.	x	
One owl hoot means everything's ok.	x	
Captain John will blow the whistle.		x

3. She and Roger had found two clues – a round place where the grass and ferns were pressed flat as if someone had been lying there and a knife.

4.

	True	False
There were many boats around the island.		x
The grass was warm from where someone had been lying.		x
Roger thinks The Swallow must be near, close to the shore.		x
John spotted the invaders first.	x	

5. The children couldn't see the invaders because they were inside their tents.

Swallows and Amazons – Summary
1. John is the leader of the four children. That is why he is called "Captain". He makes the plans and gives the orders/commands. He is probably the oldest and the most grown-up.
2. Who's There?
   The text begins with a mysterious arrow being shot at them. The children spend the entire text looking for the invaders and trying to work out who it is. It ends with the children finding

the invaders in their camp.

Swallows and Amazons – Inference
1. They were cooking. In the text, it mentions a saucepan that was over the fire.
2. They think it is the person they know who has a green parrot because the feathers on the arrow are green.
3. The Swallow is a boat. In the text it says, "landing-place" which would be where a boat is pulled up onto shore. It also says, "pulled her right up" and "drifted off" which are both things that would happen with a boat.
4. They are looking to see if there are any other boats around the island. The morning steamer would not come to their island to invade and it was far away so it didn't count in the boats they were looking for.
5. Fairly small.
   The children could call to each other when they were spread out across the island. They could hear the whistles and owl hoots. When Roger and Titty were spread apart, there was only half a dozen yards between them. It didn't take very long for them to run back to each other.
6. The invaders are dangerous – they had weapons and shot arrows at the children.
   The invaders are wild – "At that moment there was a wild yell"
   The invaders are sneaky – "The grass and ferns were pressed flat as if someone had been lying there." They had been creeping around the island trying not to be seen.

Swallows and Amazons – Prediction
1. No.
   The day turns very exciting as the children are shot at with an arrow and go looking for invaders. The day becomes an adventure.
2. Yes – the invaders have weapons and have taken over their camp.
   No – the children love their island and are determined to defend it.

Swallows and Amazons – Text Meaning
1. clue: There was a round place where the grass and ferns were pressed flat as if some one had been lying there.
   speech: "Hands up! Halt!"
   setting: There was not a sound to be heard but the quiet lapping of the water against the western shore of the island.
   action: The whole party rushed back through the trees towards the camp.
2. The dialogue moves the action forward.
   The reader finds out the children's plans through their speech.

Swallows and Amazons – Author's Use of Language
1. At that moment…
   "It's begun."
   "It may be poisoned."
2. sharp / somewhere
3. covered in forest or woods / thick and overgrown with plants / difficult to walk through / dark and shadowy
4. They are pretending to be adventurers or soldiers who have real weapons. She only has sticks but she is pretending they are pikes (real weapons).
5. The children are pretending to be soldiers so he calls out "Charge!" like the captain of an army would do.
6. It is a pirate flag which shows that they are bad characters / villains / invaders. The flag planted in the camp shows that they have claimed the camp for themselves. It is the Jolly

Roger flag which is traditionally used to identify themselves as pirates and give their victims the chance to surrender.

Swallows and Amazons – Compare and Contrast
1. Roger grabs the arrow right away but Titty is more cautious and warns Roger that it might be poisoned.
2. a) The children are called "explorers" while the invaders are "pirates".

   The children have pretend weapons (sticks) but the invaders have real weapons (bows and arrows). The children are living on the island but the others have invaded the island.

   b) Both groups want to live on the island. Both groups are trying to find / capture the other by sneaking around the island.

The Call of the Wild (pages 51–61)

The Call of the Wild – Vocabulary
1. California
2. gold
3. Northland
4. land
5. egotistical
6. inward-looking

The Call of the Wild – Retrieval
1. heavy / strong muscles / furry coats
2. swimming / to keep cool
3. Toots and Ysabel
4. playmate / guardian
5.

	True	False
Many men were travelling south.		x
Buck lived in a kennel.		x
Buck had lived at Judge Miller's place all his life.	x	
Buck liked to walk with Judge Miller's daughters, Mollie and Sarah.		x

The Call of the Wild – Summary
1. Any logical answer supported by evidence in the text, eg. He is an adventurous dog because he loves the outdoors, hunting, swimming and going for walks.

   He is the family dog because he spends time with all of the members of the Judge's family.

   He is a free dog because he can go where ever he wants – inside the house and outside.
2. King Over All

The Call of the Wild – Inference
1. He is a dog and dogs can't read.
2. Buck's life is about to change.
3. wealthy: very large house and grounds, servants, stables

   large: wide-spreading lawns, at the rear things were on even a more spacious scale than at the front, an endless and orderly array of outhouses

   posh / high class: servants, great stables, stood back from the road
4. They were not part of the family like Buck was.

   Buck was the king of all things at Judge Miller's place and they were not.

   Buck had lived there all his life while the others came and went.

The other dogs lived in the house or in kennels but he was allowed to go where he wanted.
5. He went swimming and hunting with the Judge's sons / he escorted the Judge's daughters on their walks / he lay at the Judge's feet in front of the fire / he carried the Judge's grandsons on his back / he watched over the Judge's grandsons as they played and explored.
6. to find gold (for the gold rush) / to make their fortune (get rich) / for an adventure.

The Call of the Wild – Prediction
1. companionship / protection / to pull a dog sled.
2. Children's own answers supported by evidence from the text.

The Call of the Wild – Text Meaning
1. <u>character</u>: Buck was neither a house-dog nor a kennel-dog.
   <u>warning</u>: …trouble was brewing…
   <u>setting</u>: …at the rear things were on even a more spacious scale than at the front.
   <u>action</u>: …plunged into the swimming tank…
2. Near the beginning – it introduces the main character / describes the setting / hints about something happening in the Arctic / it talks about Buck's life so far but you get the feeling it is about to change.

The Call Of The Wild – Author's Use Of Language
1. The word **legion** suggests they are like an army and the brooms and mops are their weapons.
   They are defending/protecting Toots and Ysabel from the fox terriers.
2. realm / imperiously / king overall / carried himself in a right royal fashion / aristocrat
3. country – he is used to fresh air and outdoor activities / he enjoys nature
   gentlemen – he is posh (upper class) / he is wealthy (lives a good life) / he owns or is ruler of the land
4. newspapers / servants / Klondike / steamships and transportation companies (the railways)
5. he is a part of the family / they have a special bond / they enjoy the same things

The Call of the Wild – Compare and Contrast
1. Santa Clara Valley is sunny while the Arctic is dark.
   Santa Clara Valley is warm while the Arctic is cold / frosty / frozen.
   Santa Clara Valley is south (California) while the Arctic is in the north.
2. The fox terriers are yelping and loud while Toots and Ysabel quietly look through the window.
   The fox terriers are outdoors while Toots and Ysabel are indoors.
   There are many fox terriers (at least a score – 20) while there are only two house-dogs.
3. Buck loves the outdoors and does all sorts of outdoor activities but the house-dogs rarely put a nose out of doors or set foot to the ground.
4. a) Both the Judge and his grandsons enjoy spending time with Buck.
   b) With the Judge, Buck is quiet and calm inside by the library fire but with the Judge's grandsons, Buck is playful and lively outside.
5. a) Buck is the Judge's inseparable companion just like his father.
   b) Buck is not as large as his father (because his mother was a Scotch Shepherd dog).

The Hobbit (pages 62–72)

The Hobbit – Vocabulary
1. a) like a porthole
   b) a ship
2. for longer than anyone can remember
3. rich / predictable
4. clumsy

The Hobbit – Retrieval

1.

2. Hobbits are a little people about half our height. Compared to hobbits, humans are big.
3. Ordinary everyday sort which helps them to disappear quietly and quickly.
4. natural leathery soles / covered with thick warm brown hair
5.

	True	False
Hobbits are not magical.		x
Hobbits have very good hearing.	x	
Hobbits enjoy eating.	x	
There are many hobbits in existence.		x

The Hobbit – Summary

1. Children's own answers that take into account some of the following: comfort, rooms, welcoming, well-kept, in the ground, eg. The hobbit's home is very comfortable with many rooms. It is well cared for with everything the hobbit needs.
2. Both "An Unexpected Adventure" and "A Different Sort of Hobbit" could be the correct answer. Encourage children to debate the reasons for each.
3.

	True	False
He is just like all other hobbits.		x
He always knew he'd have an adventure.		x
Hobbits are unusual creatures.	x	

The Hobbit – Inference

1. Hobbits lead a quiet life – they never had any adventures or did anything unexpected
   Hobbits get on with their neighbours – people considered them very respectable / the hobbit was fond of visitors
2. rare and shy or nervous around humans – they disappear quietly and quickly when humans are coming; happy – dress in bright colours / deep fruity laughs / good-natured faces.
3. Dislikes them / thinks they are clumsy / thinks they are not as clever as hobbits – the text calls humans stupid, large, blundering, making a noise like an elephant.
4. they are good with their hands / they are good at building things / they are good at making things
5.

	Fact	Opinion
The best rooms were all on the left-hand side.		x
He may have lost the neighbours' respect.		x
Hobbits enjoy their food.	x	
The hobbit lives in a comfortable hole.		x

The Hobbit – Prediction
1. Any two logical positive personality traits, pieces of knowledge or items with a thoughtful reason, eg. courage / confidence / new friends / strength / knowledge of the wider world.

The Hobbit – Text Meaning
1. Near the beginning – it introduces the main character / describes the setting / hints about the hobbit going on an adventure.
2. He got distracted by the need to explain what a hobbit is because the reader might not know.

The Hobbit – Author's Use of Language
1. a comfortable tunnel without smoke
   panelled walls
   floors tiled and carpeted
   polished chairs
   lots of pegs for hats and coats (for visitors)
   best rooms with windows
   windows overlooking his garden and meadows beyond
   well-to-do hobbit
2. The author wants the reader to keep reading the story to find out what happens to the hobbit. / The author wants the reader to think about what the adventure might be.
3. Hole 1 – nasty / dirty / wet / filled with worms / oozy smell
   Hole 2 – bare / sandy / nothing to sit on

The Hobbit – Compare and Contrast
1. This hobbit will have an adventure / do the unexpected whereas/but/however his ancestors never had any adventures or did anything unexpected.
2. Hobbits are smaller than dwarves.
   Hobbits have no beards whereas/but/however/while dwarves are bearded.
3. The author says humans make a noise like elephants.

Anne of Green Gables (pages 73–83)
Anne of Green Gables - Vocabulary
1. energy
2. almost empty / no one else was there
3. gravely
4. she's got a tongue of her own
5. dread / moved slowly

Anne of Green Gables – Retrieval
1. there was no sign of any train / the platform was almost deserted
2. tense rigidity / expectation / with all her might and main
3. Mrs Spencer had brought a girl instead of a boy.
4. very short, very tight ugly dress of yellowish-grey wincey / wore a faded brown sailor hat / two braids of very thick, decidedly red hair / face was small, white and thin / freckles / large mouth / large eyes / green eyes in some lights and moods and gray in others / very pointed, pronounced chin / big eyes full of spirit and vivacity / sweet-lipped, expressive mouth / broad, full forehead

5.

	True	False
Matthew paid a great deal of attention to the child waiting on the platform.		x
Mrs. Spencer told the stationmaster that Matthew and Marilla were expecting a girl from the orphan asylum.	x	
Matthew spoke first when he approached Anne.		x
Matthew told Anne there had been a mistake.		x

Anne of Green Gables – Summary

1.

Matthew discovers there's been a mistake.	3
Matthew decides to take Anne home with him.	6
Matthew approaches the girl.	4
Matthew arrives at Bright River train station	1
Anne tells Matthew all about her plan to sleep in the wild cherry-tree.	5
The stationmaster tells Matthew the 5:30 train has already been and there was a passenger dropped off for him.	2

2. Unexpected Arrival

3.

	True	False
Matthew is happy to see Anne.		x
Matthew is a confident man.		x
Anne is a chatterbox.	x	
Anne is an ordinary sort of child.		x

Anne of Green Gables – Inference
1. The stationmaster was going home for supper / the 5:30 train has been and gone / Anne is thinking about where she will spend the night.
2. He is an introverted person who doesn't like speaking to others.
3. She is good at dealing with difficult situations / she is more confident than Matthew / she takes care of problems for Matthew.
4. Anne is probably poor because her clothes are too small and worn out – "very short, very tight, very ugly dress" / "faded brown sailor hat".
5. brave – she doesn't hesitate to speak to Matthew / she wants to sleep in a cherry tree.
   chatty – she talked and talked without stopping.
   imaginative – she compares the wild cherry tree to marble halls.

Anne of Green Gables – Prediction
1. Children's own predictions supported by evidence from the text.
2. Any option is acceptable if prediction is supported by evidence from the text.

Anne of Green Gables – Text Meaning
1. <u>setting</u>: The long platform was almost deserted.
   <u>character</u>: ...answered that brisk official.
   <u>action</u>: He walked jauntily away, being hungry...
   <u>past event</u>: Mrs Spencer came off the train with that girl...

Anne of Green Gables – Author's Use of Language
1. Inspiration / things to see that will get her imagination going.
2. She thinks it would be like being in marble halls.
3. Lions are really scary so it tells the reader that Matthew is really scared of speaking to strangers.
4. She is an unusual person / She was lost (a stray) / She was part way between being a woman and a child.

Anne of Green Gables – Compare and Contrast
1. Anne is outgoing but Matthew is shy/introverted / Anne is chatty but Matthew is quiet.
2. They are both white / They are both big/large.

Black Beauty (pages 84–94)

Black Beauty – Vocabulary
1. happily
2. sturdy / firm / safe
3. awkward
4. calmed
5. The horse is well-rested.

Black Beauty – Retrieval
1. river was rising fast / many of the meadows under water / in one low part of the road the water was halfway to their knees
2. The master's business took a long time.
3. a) on the road
   b) trembling
   c) turned around to go another way
4. The horse felt sure something was wrong. He did not dare go forward.

Black Beauty – Summary
1. Children's own explanations: People think about things logically and work out answers. This can take a little while. Animals have natural instincts they follow. They don't need to think about it. They just know. Sometimes this is better because it is right and quicker. It can save people's lives.
2.

A tree branch broke off and blocked the road.	3
They all arrived home safely.	6
On a windy, autumn day, the horse took his master on a journey for business.	1
They drove back to the crossroads towards the wooden bridge.	4
The storm got worse and the river was rising.	2
Beauty refused to cross the bridge.	5

3. Humans should trust animals' instincts.

Black Beauty – Inference
1. brave: "even though he was scared, he did not turn round or run away."
   disciplined: "did not turn round or run away; I was not brought up to that."
   well-raised: "I was not brought up to that."
   frightened: "I will never say I was not frightened," / "I stopped still, and I believe I trembled."

2.

	Fact	Opinion
If they had carried on across the bridge, they would have fallen in the river.	x	
The storm was frightening.		x
Black Beauty was an animal of great value.		x
The men were very grateful to Black Beauty.	x	

3. They shouted out – "Thank God!" / "You Beauty!"
   They didn't talk for a while – "For a good while neither master nor John spoke"
   They used a serious voice – "then master began in a serious voice"
4. worried
5. thankful / grateful: "what a good supper he gave me that night… and such a thick bed of straw"
   respectful: "if your Black Beauty had not been wiser than we were"
   caring: "what a good supper he gave me that night… and such a thick bed of straw"

Black Beauty – Prediction
1. Children's own predictions supported by evidence from the text.
2. Any option is acceptable if prediction is supported by evidence from the text.

Black Beauty – Text Meaning
1. <u>setting</u>: There had been a great deal of rain…

   <u>character description</u>: John went with his master.

   <u>action</u>: …he gave me a sharp cut.

   <u>speech</u>: "I wish we were well out of this wood,"
2. Black Beauty / the horse

   Children's own responses with reference to the text.

Black Beauty – Author's Use of Language
1. It was strong / solid / safe to walk on / not too muddy
2. John had never seen such a bad storm / it was a really strong, serious storm / it was dangerous
3. groan / crack / splitting sound / tearing / crashing down / torn up by the roots / fell right across the road
4. He really wants to get their attention / he is nervous or worried / he is panicking about the storm
5. The sun had set some time / it grew darker and darker / ever since dark / we saw a light at the hall-door and at the upper windows / what a good supper he gave me that night / a thick bed of straw.

Black Beauty – Compare and Contrast
1. At the beginning, a storm is growing / starting and the leaves are blowing in the wind whereas/but/however at the end of the extract, it is calm and the storm has passed.
2. Black Beauty had a natural instinct that the river was dangerous. He refused to cross even though they told her to go on.
3. The master was quite calm but/however/whereas his wife was really worried.
4. They are both calm. They both respect the horse. They were both happy to go the long way round to stay safe.

The Secret Garden (pages 95–106)

The Secret Garden – Vocabulary
1. is skilled enough at turning the skipping rope
2. nonbelievers
3. she had to stop, was forced to stop
4. jerking
5. You ought to show me the door (today)

The Secret Garden – Retrieval
1. Digging in the kitchen-garden
2. a) key
   b) singing loudly
3. The wind blew away the ivy to show her the door to the (secret) garden.
4.

	True	False
This was the first time Mary used a skipping rope.	x	
Ben Weatherstaff gave Mary the key.		x
Mary doesn't believe in magic.		x
The wall was covered with holly.		x

The Secret Garden – Summary
1. The Secret Garden Found
2.

The robin followed Mary down the garden.	3
Mary was enjoying skipping in the garden.	1
The wind blew the ivy on the wall.	4
Mary turned the key in the lock.	6
Mary found the door to the secret garden.	5
Mary spoke with Ben Weatherstaff about her skipping.	2

3.

	True	False
Mary enjoyed skipping.	x	
Ben and Mary were friendly with each other.	x	
Mary has a lot of space in which to play.	x	
Mary hoped she would find a door for the key.	x	

The Secret Garden – Inference
1. Mary enjoys playing with it – "…she was more interested than she had ever been since she was born."
   It is good exercise for Mary – "…her cheeks were quite red"
   Mary was proud of herself – "She wanted him to see her skip."
2. She wanted him to see her skip.
3. Curious: "tha' curiosity will be th' death of thee sometime…"
   Friendly: "greeted her with a chirp."
   Helpful: "You showed me where the key was yesterday."
   Show-off: "…sang a lovely trill, merely to show off."

4. The door is here / nearby / behind the ivy.
5. Mary's heart began to thump / her hands to shake a little / in her delight and excitement/ as if he were as excited as she was.
6. She took a long, deep breath / she looked to see if anyone was coming.

The Secret Garden – Prediction
1. Any option is acceptable if prediction is supported by evidence from the text.
2. Children's own predictions supported by reasons.
3. Children's own logical predictions supported by reasons.

The Secret Garden – Text Meaning
1. character: ...and he opened his beak and sang a loud, lovely trill, merely to show off.
   dialect: P'raps tha' art a young 'un, after all...
   speech: "You showed me where the key was yesterday," she said,
   action: ...and suddenly a gust of wind swung aside some loose ivy trails...

The Secret Garden – Author's Use of Language
1. Perhaps she was grumpy or sad / in a bad mood. She wasn't very active and acted like an adult instead of a child.
2. wonderful / interested / delightful / laugh / pleasure
3. It is attached at the top but not at the bottom. It hangs down like a curtain. It is thick and covers the wall. It can be moved aside.
4. rusty / old / stiff / difficult to open
5. secretive / mysterious – "…looked behind her up the long walk to see if anyone was coming."
   suspense / tense / nervous – "the door which opened slowly – slowly."
   excited – "breathing quite fast with excitement, and wonder, and delight."

The Secret Garden – Compare and Contrast
1. At the beginning, Mary is happy with her skipping whereas/but/however at the end of the extract, she is feeling curious and mysterious about where the door leads.
2. Mary and the robin are both happy/cheerful/excited and enjoy each other's company.
3. Any traditional tale involving magic (Aladdin because the magical genie grants wishes.)
4. Any logical moment with a reason to back up the answer (When the wind lifts the ivy to reveal the door. It is very mysterious and magical.)

The Jungle Book (pages 107–120)

The Jungle Book – Vocabulary
1. refuses to allow
2. diseased
3. checked
4. quarry
5. exhausted / tired / worked-up / agitated
6. acceptance

The Jungle Book – Retrieval
1. They become mangy and lose their teeth.
2. He went to bound before he saw what he was jumping at and needed to stop. He didn't want to leap on the man's cub.
3. Looked up into Father Wolf's face and laughed.
4. He had burnt his feet in a fire.
5. They must show him to the (wolf) pack.

6.

	True	False
The wolves heard Shere Khan capture his prey.		x
Father Wolf attacked the animal rustling in the bushes.		x
The man's cub was wearing clothes.		x
Shere Khan came right into the wolves' cave.		x

The Jungle Book – Summary
1. Any clear summary that links to the first paragraph. If animals kill humans, eventually men will come into the jungle to hunt the animals.
2. Unafraid: (Any logical explanation with reference to the next.) For example: The text is all about how bold and brave the man's cub is even though he is lost in the jungle; being chased by a tiger and taken in by wolves. Mother Wolf is unafraid when she protects Mowgli from Shere Khan.

The Jungle Book – Inference
1. To protect all of the animals / So some animals don't do things that put all of the animals in danger.
2. fearless: He laughed at a dangerous wolf.

   naïve/unknowing: he didn't know that the wolf could hurt him.
3. No

   He is being sarcastic. The text says, "but his eyes were very angry." He sounds like he is being respectful but his eyes show that he is really angry with Shere Khan.
4. She is showing that she is stronger than him.

   To embarrass him / belittle him / make fun of him.
5. respectful
6. strong: she stands up to Shere Khan.
   clever/cunning: she knows what to say to make him go away / embarrass.
   has a bad side: you wouldn't want to mess with her.
   ferocious: she would fight for the man's cub.

The Jungle Book – Prediction
1. He will grow up to hunt Shere Khan.
2. If Shere Khan had killed the man's cub, the villagers would have hunted through all the animals' lairs in revenge.

The Jungle Book – Text Meaning
1. <u>character</u>: Then there was a howl – an untigerish howl – .

   <u>speech</u>: "Ye choose and ye do not choose!"

   <u>setting</u>: The moonlight was blocked out of the mouth of the cave...

   <u>action</u>: Father Wolf ran out a few paces and heard Shere Khan muttering and mumbling savagely...
2. To show that Shere Khan intends to break the Law of the Jungle.

   To show that the wolves are following the Law of the Jungle.

   To show the relationship / community of the animals in the jungle and that Shere Khan is not a part of that community.

The Jungle Book – Author's Use of Language
1. "Untigerish" shows that he may not be as tough as he seems / he isn't really a strong, fierce tiger.
2. He laughed in the face of Father Wolf.

   He pushed his way between the cubs to get close to the warm hide.

© Brilliant Publications Limited

Classic Children's Literature Years 5–6

He started eating with the other baby wolves (had milk from Mother Wolf).
3. To insult Shere Khan / striped, meaning the tiger, and cattle-killer shows that he kills animals that are easy prey.
4. Lame means not able to walk properly. Babies can't walk when they are first born. Shere Khan can't walk properly because he burned his feet in the fire. The author is comparing Shere Khan to when he was a baby.
5. (The cub is mine, and) to my teeth he will come in the end
6. Hairless / lively / energetic / bouncy

The Jungle Book – Compare and Contrast
1. They tell each other that there is no pride in killing men. They are easy to kill so it isn't a big success to kill them. They won't look strong if they kill men.
2. a) Mother Wolf's eyes were like two green moons in the darkness while Shere Khan's were blazing. Blazing sounds like fire so his eyes were yellow, red or orange.
   Mother Wolf's eyes were like moons while Shere Khan's eyes were blazing like the sun.
   b) They are both bright.
   They are both staring straight at the other.
3. Raksha means Demon and is strong but/while Lungri means Lame One and is weak.
4. Mother Wolf thinks the man's cub will grow up to hunt Shere Khan as Shere Khan has hunted the man's cub.

Treasure Island (pages 121–131)

Treasure Island – Vocabulary
1. location
2. lodging
3. connoisseur
4. a pub in a good location
5. horse-drawn coach

Treasure Island – Retrieval
1. There is still treasure on the island and he doesn't want anyone to find it.
2. tall / strong / heavy / nut-brown / tarry pigtail / soiled blue coat / hands ragged and scarred / black, broken nails / sabre cut across one cheek / old, tottering voice
3.

	True	False
The seaman was on his own when he arrived at the inn.		x
The seaman had a scar on his face.	x	
The seaman chose the inn because it was popular.		x
The narrator was paid a silver fourpenny each week to watch out for the man with one leg.		x

4. a) Admiral Benbow   b) sabre
   c) captain   d) watched for ships

Treasure Island – Summary

1.

The old seaman spent time at the cove and upon the cliffs with his telescope.	5
The old seaman arrived at the inn.	2
The old seaman gave the innkeeper gold pieces to pay for his room and food.	4
The old seaman arrived in the town to look for a suitable inn.	1
The narrator had nightmares about the man with one leg.	6
The old seaman asked about the popularity of the inn.	3

2.

	True	False
The narrator was a bit afraid of the old seaman.	x	
The seaman was nervous around strangers.	x	
The seaman was like all the other guests at the inn.		x
Thoughts of the old seaman caused nightmares for the narrator.		x

Treasure Island – Inference

1. He didn't want to be found.
2. Look through the door before entering.
   Be as silent as a mouse when any other seafaring men were present.
3. He was a silent man.
   He would not speak when spoken to.
   He asked if any seafaring men had gone by along the road.
   He looked in through the curtain before entering the parlour.
   He was as silent as a mouse when any other seafaring men were present.
   He was on the look out for the seafaring man with one leg.
4. Intrigued / interested – he helped him look out for the seafaring man with one leg.
   Frightened – "How that personage haunted my dreams"
5. The narrator had never actually seen the man with one leg so he didn't know what he looked like. Because the old seaman seemed to be worried about him, the narrator worried too.

Treasure Island – Prediction

1. Children's own predictions supported by evidence from the text.
2. Any option is acceptable if prediction is supported by evidence from the text.

Treasure Island – Text Meaning

1. speech: ...keep my 'weather-eye open for a seafaring man with one leg'.
   setting: On stormy nights, when the wind shook the four corners of the house...
   action: ...he drank slowly, like a connoisseur, lingering on the taste...
   character: ...his hands ragged and scarred, with black, broken nails

Treasure Island – Author's Use of Language

1. He's a pirate – "dead man's chest" is treasure and pirates look for treasure.
   He's a pirate – "Yo-ho-ho" is something pirates say.
   violent / dangerous – "dead man's chest" Has he killed someone?
2. Simile: looking as fierce as a commander
   This suggests that he is stern / someone to listen to / demands respect and obedience / in charge.

Simile: as silent as a mouse
This suggests he doesn't want to be heard / he is sneaking around / he is hiding from someone.

3. had none of the appearance of a man who sailed before the mast / he seemed like a mate or skipper
4. haunted / diabolical / monstrous / creature / nightmare / abominable
5. He worked hard for the money. He paid with fear and worry.

Treasure Island – Compare and Contrast
1. Any option is acceptable if answer is supported by evidence from the text.
2. At the beginning of the paragraph, the narrator thought the seaman was looking for other seamen to spend time with whereas/but/however at the end of the paragraph, the narrator realises the old seaman is trying to avoid other seafaring men.

Twenty Thousand Leagues Under the Sea (pages 132–145)

Twenty Thousand Leagues Under the Sea – Vocabulary
1. Semi-darkness between daylight and darkness / the last bits of sunlight were shining in the sky.
2. a) utterly inaccessible
   b) feasible
   c) instinct
   d) gouge
   e) continually
3. counterweight
4. leaning

Twenty Thousand Leagues Under the Sea – Retrieval
1. the Southern Cross
   polar star
2. walruses — go beneath the Ice Bank to find more feasible seas
   birds — migrate northward to escape the cold
   seals — gouge holes in the ice fields so they can breathe
   whales — accustomed to staying on the icy waterways
3. seals and walruses
4. a) five and a half months
   b) 14,000 leagues / longer than the earth's equator
5. a violent collision
6.

	True	False
The glass cases had fallen over in the collision.		X
This is the first time the Nautilus had gone aground.		X
The Nautilus was still moving slowly.		X
The Nautilus was leaning to its starboard side.	X	

7. The block of ice is rising with it, stopping the Nautilus from regaining balance.
8. He is worried they will hit the bottom of the Ice Bank and be crushed/squeezed between the two blocks of ice.

Twenty Thousand Leagues Under the Sea – Summary
1.

The author reflected on his time at sea.	3
They tried to find out what had caused the collision.	5
The Nautilus sank beneath the ice.	2
They were worried they would become trapped in the ice bank and the piece of ice beneath them.	6
The people on board the Nautilus were woken suddenly.	4
The crew of the Nautilus prepared to depart the Antarctic region.	1

2. An iceberg toppled over because it had eroded at the bottom. A piece of ice hit the Nautilus. It slid under the submarine and pushed it up causing it to stop and lean over.
3. An Antarctic Accident

Twenty Thousand Leagues Under the Sea – Inference
1. Winter is coming and the ice is getting thicker.
2. A submarine – it sinks / it moves underwater with a propeller / it has a ballast tank for moving up and down.
3. amazed / fortunate / positive / wonderful / overwhelmed

   Evidence: completely wrapped up in his memories / reached that inaccessible spot without facing exhaustion or danger / wondering if the rest of the journey will have comparable surprises / series of underwater wonders / so many fascinating or frightening incidents / memories crossed over from one dream to the next / not giving his brain a moment's rest
4. He thought the submarine had run aground at the surface of the sea. He was surprised they were still so far under water.
5. Captain Nemo was anxious about the situation – in the text, it says he revealed a certain uneasiness.

   Captain Nemo was a man of few words – he gave very short answers to questions. Captain Nemo was very intelligent – he was using the instruments to work out what had happened / he was philosophising about what had happened.

Twenty Thousand Leagues Under the Sea – Prediction
1. Yes
   The author must have lived to tell the story and share all of his notes from their adventures. They ran aground in the past and made it out (the Canadian said, "I don't think it'll pull through like that first time in the Torres Strait.")
   or
   No
   It might hit the underbelly of the Ice Bank and be hideously squeezed between the two frozen surfaces.
   The Canadian doesn't think it'll pull through like the first time in the Torres Strait.
2. Yes – he has had many fascinating adventures on the Nautilus. He has been to many amazing places.
   No – some of his adventures have been frightening. They had faced exhaustion and danger during the voyage.

Twenty Thousand Leagues Under the Sea – Text Meaning
1. The author wants to describe the setting: the temperature, the sky, the animals. He is showing the reader why they need to leave the Antarctic (colder weather and more ice is coming).
2. In the middle – They have already been travelling for a long time but they need to try to escape from the ice so there is still more story to come.

Twenty Thousand Leagues Under the Sea – Author's Use of Language
1. "The last gleams of twilight were melting into night." – The word twilight means the time of day between daylight and darkness.
   The stars can be seen in the sky even though it's six o'clock in the morning – "The wonderful Southern Cross, polar star of the Antarctic regions, twinkled at its zenith."
2. -12 degrees centigrade
   sharp nip in the air
   ice floes were increasing
   the sea was starting to congeal
   numerous black patches were spreading over its surface
   imminent formation of fresh ice
   the southernmost basin froze
   beneath the Ice Bank
   harshest climate
   icy waterways
   escape the cold
   polar continent
3. He is a scientist or a researcher.
   "I spent the day putting my notes into final form."
4. as if our seagoing passenger carriage had glided there on railroad tracks
5. It is unstoppable / more powerful than anything. It is overpowering / invincible.

Twenty Thousand Leagues Under the Sea – Compare and Contrast
1. The ice block above the ship is like a hard tortoise shell. It might be curved like a dome over the top of them.
2. Captain Nemo is very calm and thoughtful. He doesn't say very much. He only explains the details about what has happened. On the other hand, the Canadian shouts and has an outburst, blowing off steam. He complains and says he thinks they won't pull through.
3. In the story, they used a compass, map and pressure gauge. These items are still used today but they are on computers and much more high-tech. Now, all of the instruments are electronic and give much more detail about the area around a ship. Now, sailors may have been able to predict the iceberg turning over and stay out of danger. In the story, they didn't have any way of knowing it was going to happen.

A Christmas Carol (pages 146–158)

A Christmas Carol – Vocabulary
1. without doubt
2. He was Marley's only friend. He was the only person bothered about Marley's death.
3. tight-fisted
4. Focus on working hard at one's job.
5. He has white hair. He is old.
6. Being blind is better than being Scrooge (mean).

A Christmas Carol – Retrieval
1. The register of his burial had been signed by lots of official people.
2. (our) ancestors
3. Nothing wonderful can come of the story.
4.

5.

	True	False
Children would ask Scrooge for the time.		x
Scrooge walked along the sides of the crowds.	x	
This story takes place in Autumn.		x
The city was covered in a thick fog.	x	

6. He didn't ask Scrooge for more coal because he was afraid he might lose his job.
7. It is a time for paying bills without money.

A Christmas Carol – Summary
1. Any clear summary that includes the key points:
   Marley was dead.
   Scrooge was cold-hearted.
   It was Christmas Eve.
   Scrooge and his nephew don't agree about Christmas.
2. Frosty and Friendless.
   Scrooge was cold-hearted and the weather was cold. (Any relevant quotes as evidence.)
   Scrooge was all alone in the world with no friends. (Any relevant quotes as evidence.)

A Christmas Carol – Inference
1. He was not all that upset. "Scrooge was not so dreadfully cut up by the sad event."
2. He had made a good deal / got a good price. "…he was an excellent man of business on the very day of the funeral, and solemnised it with an undoubted bargain."
3. ghost
4. no warmth
   chill
   bitterer
   foul
   wintry
5. unfriendly
   poor
   anti-social
(Any relevant quotes from this paragraph)

A Christmas Carol – Prediction
1. Yes – reference to no friends, cold-hearted, he was cruel to his clerk.
   No – He has a nephew. He might join him for Christmas and change his ways.
2. Yes – Marley might be a ghost like the reference to Hamlet's father.
   Scrooge might die alone like Marley.

A Christmas Carol – Text Meaning
1. <u>metaphor</u>: from which no steel had ever struck out a generous fire
   <u>simile</u>: dead as a door-nail
   <u>setting</u>: of all the good days in the year, on Christmas Eve
   <u>character</u>: he was all in a glow; his face was ruddy and handsome
2. Charles Dickens (the author)
3. He doesn't like him. He is very critical of Scrooge.

A Christmas Carol – Author's Use of Language
1. as dead as a doornail

2. A coffin is for dead bodies so it makes more sense for a coffin-nail to be used in this simile.
3. tight-fisted / sinner / sharp / hard / covetous / squeezing / wrenching / grasping / scraping /clutching / cold / shrewdly / grating
4. The setting is cold and bleak. This contributes to the mood of the story which is dark and cold. The description of the cold weather outside makes the reader feel cold and negative.
5. Pudding and holly are associated with Christmas; which is about being jolly, happy and kind but Scrooge is talking about them as a way to hurt people.

A Christmas Carol – Compare and Contrast
1. Any logical answer with reference to the text. (Scrooge reminds me of The Grinch Who Stole Christmas because they are both cold-hearted and they don't think anyone should be happy at Christmas.)
2. fire
3. flint
4. Scrooge's nephew is extremely happy / cheerful / positive, however/while/but Scrooge is angry / cross / negative.
5. Scrooge is saying a person has to be rich to be happy. He says his nephew shouldn't be merry because he is poor.

Acknowledgements

Little House in the Big Woods by Laura Ingalls-Wilder *(Harper, 1932)*
Chapter 6 from Little House in the Big Woods by Laura Ingalls Wilder, © text copyright 1932, 1960 Little House Heritage Trust. Illustrated By: Garth Williams. Used by permission of HarperCollins Publishers

The Lion, the Witch and the Wardrobe by C.S. Lewis copyright
© C.S Lewis Pte. Ltd. 1950
Extract reprinted by permission.

Swallows and Amazons by Arthur Ransom *(Jonathan Cape, 1930)*
Extract from Swallows and Amazons by Arthur Ransome published by Red Fox, copyright © 2001. Reproduced by permission of The Random House Group Ltd Ltd and David R. Godine, Publisher, Boston, Massachusetts

The Call of the Wild by Jack London (Macmillan, 1903)

The Hobbit by J.R.R. Tolkien (George Allen & Unwin, 1937)
Copyright © The Tolkien Estate Limited, 1937, 1951, 1966, 1978, 1995. Reprinted by permission of HarperCollins Publishers Ltd

Anne of Green Gables by Lucy Maud Montgomery (L.C. Page & Co, 1908)

Black Beauty by Anna Sewell (Jarrold & Sons, 1877)

The Secret Garden by Frances Hodgson Burnett (Frederick A. Stokes, 1911)

The Jungle Book by Rudyard Kipling (Macmillan, 1894)

Treasure Island by Robert Louis Stevenson (Cassell and Co, 1883)

Twenty Thousand Leagues Under the Sea by Jules Verne (Pierre-Jules Hetzel, 1872)

A Christmas Carol by Charles Dickens (Chapman & Hall, 1843)

References

English Reading Test Framework, National Curriculum Tests from 2016, 2016 Key Stage 2 English Reading Test Framework: National Curriculum Tests from 2016 Electronic version product code: STA/15/7341/e ISBN: 978-1-78315-826-3

The National Curriculum in England: Key Stage 1 and 2 framework document, December 2014, Reference: DFE-00177-2013

www.ingramcontent.com/pod-product-compliance
Lightning Source LLC
Chambersburg PA
CBHW081357160426
43192CB00013B/2432